JOHN W. BECKER
1100 Wilson
Norfolk, Neb. 68701

YOUR PASTOR'S PROBLEMS

YOUR PASTOR'S PROBLEMS

A Guide for Ministers and Laymen

by

William E. Hulme

1966

DOUBLEDAY & COMPANY, INC.

GARDEN CITY, NEW YORK

The author acknowledges with thanks permission to use
material from "Binker" from the book *Now We Are Six*
by A. A. Milne. Copyright, 1927, by E. P. Dutton & Co.,
Inc. Renewal, © 1955, by A. A. Milne. Reprinted by
permission of E. P. Dutton & Co., Inc., Methuen & Co.,
Ltd., and Mr. C. R. Milne.

To my
Father and Mother
in gratitude
for a Christian home

CONTENTS

YOUR PASTOR'S PROBLEMS

I. THE CRISIS

In an article addressed to clergymen entitled "Preacher's Dictionary," Bishop Gerald Kennedy attempts to translate the special vocabulary that laymen may use in reference to their pastors. He offers the "dictionary" in the hope that it may be a "useful and practical guide for young men entering the ministry" in "comprehending the often obscure speech of some laymen." The dictionary consists of the following lay references to the pastor together with the definitions.

"He is a spiritual preacher"
    (He never disturbs me)
"He is not a spiritual preacher"
    (His message is too relevant)
"He brings politics into the pulpit"
    (I do not agree with him)
"He speaks out with courage"
    (I agree with him)
"He is pink"
    (He dares to criticize the status quo)
"His position will hurt the church"
    (We reactionaries are displeased)
"His attitude will hurt church finance"
    (I will cut my subscription from 25 cents per week to 5)
"I will not remain in the church"
    (If I cannot rule, I'll quit)
"He is sowing dissension"
    (Some people are waking up)
"He must consider his position"
    (I want an emasculated citizen in the pulpit)

"He is after the money"
> (He thinks his family should have an American standard of
> living)

"He has a great future"
> (He is a politician)

"His ministry is successful"
> (The church has subscribed the budget)

"He lacks judgment"
> (He takes Jesus seriously)

"He neglects the substantial member"
> (The church is beginning to move)

"He plays up to the new members"
> (He is bypassing the road blocks we set up)

"He will ruin us financially"
> (The tightwads have a guilty conscience)

"At least he is a good pastor"
> (He can't preach)

"He disturbs me"
> (I am beginning to grow spiritually)

"He upsets my faith"
> (My prejudices are taking a beating)

"The whole church is upset"
> (I am causing all the trouble I can)[1]

One catches quite easily in these definitions the image
the pastor has of the layman—or at least the image he has of
the layman's image of the pastor. One could not expect the
challenge to go unnoticed. In the correspondence in a subsequent issue there was a reply entitled "Preacher's Language," in which the writer offered the following list of
preacherisms with interpretations "for the benefit of the lay
reader."

"It has been the teaching of the church down through the centuries . . ." (The Early Fathers taught this, but it doesn't make
sense to me.)

"The consensus of modern theological thinking is . . ." (One of
my seminary professors said . . .)

"An interesting solution was recently proposed by a leading theologian." (I saw a book review that said something about this.)

"In the words of the poet . . ." (I can't remember which poet wrote this.)

"Another engagement prevents me from attending the banquet." (I can't afford a pair of tickets right now.)

"Our beloved bishop strongly recommends . . ." (If we don't do this, I'll be in hot water.)

"I have some material on that subject in my study." (Next month I'm going to work up a filing system.)

"I feel it is my duty to serve on this important commission." (Maybe I'll make some good contacts at those meetings.)

"Everyone owes it to himself to secure sufficient rest." (How I hate to get up in the morning.)[2]

What is expressed in this lighthearted give-and-take is the age-old feud between the clergy and the laity—a feud that has reached a critical point. A few years back we were hearing much about ministers who were breaking down. Now we are hearing about ministers who are quitting the ministry. The same conflict is behind both phenomena—and it is a conflict that involves the layman. This book addresses itself to this mutual crisis. It is directed to pastor and layman together because it is a problem that concerns them both. The interpretations of each other's speech—while offered with a sense of humor—is indicative of a breakdown in communication between these two groups in the Church. For many laymen the pastor lives in a world apart, and for many pastors, the layman fails to grasp the real significance of the Gospel.

Perhaps the freedom to "quit" is the big difference today. The ministry is something like marriage. In a former day people who were not happily married probably would stay together because divorce was not the accepted thing. Today they would be divorced because the stigma is gone. So in a former day ordination was for life. Men who were unhappy in the ministry stuck it out because to demit was not the accepted thing. Today, particularly if he is young, he may quit.

The Layman's Basic Problem: The Image of Authority

The basic problem in the layman's attitude toward the clergy concerns the clergyman as an authority figure. The minister himself may not want to be an authority. Yet, by the very nature of his office he cannot escape this image. Because he has a special position of leadership in the congregation, he has the aura of authority.

Most of us have ambivalent feelings toward authority. When our feelings are negative the authority represents a privileged position that we resent and may even attack. Typical of this antagonism is a letter to the editor of a denominational publication by a layman who showed his irritation at the clergy by sarcastically referring to them as our *gutsy* pastors.[3] As we might expect there was a later letter from a pastor deploring this "new low in describing our pastors and church leaders."[4]

Problems over authority exist also in the clerical structure itself. I am sure that Bishop Kennedy knows that pastors also have a special vocabulary for bishops. Even the pope, whose authority is fortified by infallibility, is not spared. When he refused to intervene in the decision of the Council presidents to postpone the vote on the issue of religious liberty in the third session of Vatican Council II, Father John Courtney Murray, who was a leading influence in the shaping of the religious liberty proposal, was asked by the press if he was disappointed in the pope's action. "Disappointment would not be enough," said Father Murray. "Resentment would not be too strong a word."[5]

When the church council of a Protestant congregation in this country was questioning itself concerning the difficulty of the congregation in securing a pastor, one of the members asked, "Hasn't this church usually gone along with the minister—given him what he wants?" One of the veterans of the congregation agreed. "In my family the father was the head of the home. We have always thought of the minister in the same way in the congregation." While this man obviously had a great deal of respect for his father, the chances are that this respect was mixed with resentment. Men sense a competitive threat with other men, even with those who are supposedly in authority. Lacking this competitive approach, the women in the congregation can view the masculine authority of the minister with more unequivocal admiration. For those more aggressive women who are in revolt against male domination—and their number seems to be decreasing —the ministerial authority presents a threat. They can attack it as well as any man.

The authority of the minister is complicated by the fact that he is considered a *moral* authority. He is the *preacher* and his very presence can make people feel guilty. Even ministers themselves tend to accept this connotation of preaching. When a member of a local ministerium began to remonstrate with his brethren over certain laxities in their practice, one of his brethren interrupted by saying, "Don't preach to *me*." Preaching, thus, is associated with moralizing—or even worse, moral rebuking. This is ironic since according to the Christian heritage the preacher is the herald of "good news." His function in preaching is not to make people feel guilty, but to proclaim the love and power of God.

The authority of the minister does not have to be resented to have a negative effect in congregational life. Some people are attracted to his authority in a desire to share in his status. They seek to obtain his favor by supporting his authority in the hope of securing a special attachment to him. Should others seem to have the "inside track," they feel personally rejected and become jealous of their "competitors."

The Clergyman's Complaint

The clergyman's complaint against the layman is that he identifies his Christianity with his culture—and this complaint has become increasingly vocal. In the fall of 1964 the Episcopal Church in convention had before it a resolution to support people who participate in demonstrations for civil rights even though they be forbidden to do so by local laws. The House of Bishops approved the measure while the House of Deputies, composed of laymen as well as clergy, defeated it, the majority of the laymen voting against it. The day following this defeat in the House of Deputies, an Episcopal clergyman preaching at Bond Chapel at the University of Chicago said that he had always favored increased participation of the layman in the life of the Church, but after this decision against "obeying God rather than man," he had his serious misgivings. The layman is seen as a brake on the witness of the Church—a social and political conservative who sanctifies the *status quo*. There are laymen who actually push the pastor for a more radical Christian witness. But these are usually a minority in any congregation. Their presence is often an indication of a power struggle within the congregation as much as a judgment upon the clergyman. One of these is Mrs. Lucy Montgomery, a prominent churchwoman in the Episcopal Church and a worker for progressive community concerns. Recently she caused a stir by quitting the Church—the counterpart to the minister's quitting the ministry. Her greatest disappointment, she said, was her failure to get her pastor and her fellow churchwomen to sign petitions against nuclear testing. "I was terribly concerned and still am. And neither the clergy nor the women thought it was their place to speak up. I was all alone."[6]

When I was teaching a class of lay leaders, I asked them to describe the potential of their congregations. One of them wrote, "The church to which I belong is outwardly one that must be called successful. The pastor's policy is to keep all groups satisfied, to avoid any open issues or conflicts, and to keep the congregation happy with itself and isolated from the Church at large. Preaching is generally limited to inspirational and nonirritating sermons. It is a pleasant respectable church family, busy with its own affairs, but not concerned with taking Christ to others, even within the immediate community. Can they or should they be stirred up by a change of pastoral leadership? Or can the laymen of the congregation get it off dead center?"

When the conflict worsens, the minister may view the layman's intransigence as a type of persecution. In a recent book, *Neurotics in the Church,* the clergyman-author says that "the dedicated preacher will have more enemies within the church than without." The clergyman identifies these enemies as the lay leaders in the congregation who want to control the congregation. These "power-mad laymen" are seen as threats not only to the pastor's authority, but, as the indigestible obstacle in this neurotic power struggle, they may actually oust the pastor. What is needed is the strengthening of church discipline to oust these lay troublemakers after all else fails. "We cannot have Protestant freedom," he says, "without authority."[7]

The anonymous Presbyterian minister who created something of a sensation by his article "Why I Quit the Ministry" in the *Saturday Evening Post* places the cause for his departure squarely upon the layman.

I still believe in Jesus Christ. I still want to serve Him. For it is He who taught me to care—about man, God, and the deepest questions of life. This is why I quit the ministry. The majority of today's church members refuse to care. In this refusal, most remaining members and much of their chosen church hierarchy blandly acquiesce. How then can a minister rationalize devoting his life to the organization which results, a superficial extension of society? How can he live with himself if he does?[8]

The problem is not confined to the American Church. Writing in a Canadian magazine, a former minister of the United Church of Canada tells why most Protestant churches are losing some of their best ministers. "The congregation expects you to be a theological chartered accountant—dull, conservative, ultra-pietistic, and above all, uncontroversial." He sees in the restrictions against a minister's drinking and smoking the symptom of a larger disease —"the tendency of congregations to regard their minister as a hired professional Christian, someone they pay to forego the vices they're unwilling to forego themselves."[9] And so he quit the ministry to work in public relations.

The Enviable Layman

When I wrote to our student intern in a university church to solicit his help in interesting qualified students in the ministry, he replied that his interest was only lukewarm. "I envy the layman," he wrote. "He doesn't have to bother with all the junk that encumbers the minister." It is ironic that by *junk* he meant the lay activities in the congregation. The criticism of the laity has its concealed envy. This envy is almost always directed toward the layman's participation in the world rather than lay activity within the organizational framework of the Church. Wayne Oates expressed this envy in unequivocal terms. "I am an ordained Baptist minister," he says, "but I am beginning to feel the need to be ordained as a layman too! I have come to 'cast a sidelong glance of envy' at the layman's ministry with just that same sense of 'the laying on of hands' that I have about being a clergyman." And what is this layman's ministry according to Oates? It is the doctor making house calls, the psychologist helping the discouraged, the teacher with his pupils, the country-store operator with his wise counsel for the distressed.[10]

But what the layman does in terms of organized lay activity is likely to be looked down upon rather than envied. The group that takes the brunt of this criticism is the "Ladies' Society." To those who wish to poke fun at the local congregation, the ladies' group represents the epitome of inconsequential activity. Unfortunately its "society page" activities often merit this judgment, although almost on any basis for judgment, the men's group would fare even worse. Also if the minister is honest he will admit that the ladies' group is pretty much what the male clergy of the church has wanted it to be. Why pick on it then? Could it not be that, although the male leadership of the church has seen to it that women stay out of the governing bodies of the churches, in their supposedly harmless activities these women have become the real power of the local congregation?

The Old Battle of the Sexes

What pastor has not had his times of fear and trepidations about facing the ladies concerning the disposal of their "well-heeled" treasury or on the use of the church parlors? A man's mother conflict is usually more ambiguous than his father conflict, and the church ladies' group is often quite motherly. In fact the religious life itself is predominately mother-centered. The Church is referred to as Mother Church. It was to an assembly of nuns that Pope Paul VI announced that he was giving Mary the honorary title of Mother of the Church. This action prompted a Mexican bishop to pose the observation that if the Church is our mother, and Mary is the Mother of the Church, then Mary must in reality be our grandmother. It would appear at least that the women are being given their due. Could the male tendency to make light of the church women's group be an expression of the old battle between the sexes in which the power struggle is rarely faced because of obvious ambivalences and dependencies?

The Real Loss of Clergy Status

The situation with which we are confronted today is not simply an old feud. The office of the ministry is in a crisis. One manifestation of this crisis is the low ebb in the pastoral image. The number of students studying for the ministry is declining. Many of those who are attending theological seminaries are hoping to avoid the parish ministry. As these threats became critical the Interseminary Movement—a student group—asked Walter Wagoner—a veteran in theological education—to assess the situation. In the result of this study—a book entitled *Bachelor of Divinity: Uncertain Servants in Seminary and Ministry*—Wagoner quotes Heinrich Vogel to the effect that in choosing the ministry, "one chooses to man an outpost of unequaled danger which threatens not only from without, but also from within."[11] I myself have visited many church-related colleges during the past few years in the interest of the seminary and have discovered that the image of the pretheological student on these campuses is not very attractive. Some students prefer to keep their intentions regarding the ministry to themselves in order to avoid being classified in this category. This represents a change of status for the pretheological student since I taught in a church-related college a decade ago.

The minister suffers from a sense of professional inferiority. In his own mind he is the low man on the professional totem pole. This is a psychiatric age. We have witnessed a shift from religion to medicine in the ills of the soul. The minister feels he compares unfavorably to the doctor. With timidity (if at all) he approaches the doctor concerning his own parishioners. Granger Westberg, a well-known pastoral theologian, has raised a provocative question. "What would have happened if Sigmund Freud had been a rabbi instead of a doctor?" A successor to Freud, Viktor Frankl, has made a similar observation. "Some of the people who nowadays call on a psychiatrist would have seen a pastor, priest, or rabbi in former days," he says, "but now they often refuse to be handed over to a clergyman, so that the doctor is confronted with philosophical questions rather than emotional conflicts."[12] The minister's loss of prestige is that of one who used to be on the inside and now stands outside looking in.

The switch has gone so far that ministers invite the psychiatrist to teach them how to conduct their own pastoral care. Some seminaries call in the psychiatrist for the same purpose. In contrast, it is rare indeed for a minister ever to address a group of physicians. Even if he had the opportunity, he would not be audacious enough to advise them concerning the effective treatment of their patients. The minister is the object of everybody's education program. Mental health departments, state universities, and even morticians plan conferences for him.

Guilt about Professional Inferiority

The minister's professional inferiority is further aggravated by the bombardment he receives from his denominational headquarters. Each of the departmental executives wants to inform him concerning the improvement of his ministry. The impression left upon the minister is that he is always hearing about what he is *not* doing. His sins of omission, it seems, are legion. It is relatively easy to make a minister feel guilty. His religious temperament sensitizes him to the magnitude of his responsibilities and to his shortcomings. When I discussed this professional inferiority with a group of ministers, one of them said, "It is not just that the minister feels inferior, he *is* inferior." When I asked him why he felt this way he said, "When I listen to these psychiatrists I know that I have not had the training necessary to minister effectively to people in need." He was attacking his seminary education. Some seminaries have indeed been lax in keeping up with the developments in pastoral care, particularly in its clinical dimensions, and their graduates keenly feel the lack. However, the trend is in the other direction and more and more seminaries are incorporating the clinical aspects into their core curriculum in pastoral theology.

The pastoral image has been further depleted by the scientific emphasis of our day. Ever since Sputnik we have intensified our scientific race with Russia, and as so often happens we have adopted some of the attitudes as well as the goals of our competitor. Khrushchev called priests black-robed devils and said they ought to be put to work. There is not much justification for the "work" of the ministry in terms of scientific progress. In fact, his role is superfluous —a direct descendant of the archaic "goldbricker," the shaman, whose value in production stands in contrast to that of the worker. From the value standards of our times the question concerning whether the minister is really needed is valid. Can the sacred with its nonutilitarian nature any longer justify its existence—particularly a sacred professional? The minister is raising this question himself. The seminary student is also asking it. Why bother? Why need we defend it—what is there really to defend? Is this structure of a minister to a congregation really necessary? Or is it time to scrap the whole thing in search for a more effective way of ministry, whatever that may be?

Beyond Study to Action

This brings us back to the layman—for the pastor-layman relationship is at the center of the crisis. No matter how much we may emphasize the lay ministry and no matter how envious the pastor may be of this ministry, the fact remains that, without the ministry of the clergy, the lay ministry would not long survive. Walter Wagoner is very direct at this point. "There is no surer way of nurturing heresy and obscurantism within Christianity than to abolish a paid specially educated professional leadership. . . . Without it atrophy will set in. . . . A vigorous and competent professional ministry is the right supplement to a strong laity."[13] Though he represents the Society of Friends which has traditionally questioned any marked division between lay and clergy, Elton Trueblood shows this same concern when he says, "The Christian ideal is that of the universal or lay ministry but this ideal cannot be realized unless there are men who specialize in making it real."[14] Even Peter Berger, a critic of the institutional Church, would probably concur. In his advice to a young man who asked whether he should study for the parish ministry, Berger replied, "Should you become a parish minister? I don't know. But somehow I hope so—a little. . . . It is persons such as you who show promise of becoming what I hope to find when I go into a church—ministers who know fully the tenuousness of their performance and who yet find it in themselves to carry it on, and to do so on my behalf."[15] It would seem to be a fact that, if we are going to have any ministry as such, the office and authority of a particular ministry is indispensable.

But in what does this leadership consist? Is it not to lead the laity in a united front in meeting the world? The Church is in the world and it is to the world that it must witness. For this encounter we must go from the pew to the market place. What happens to this marshaling of our lay forces if the leader's problems in relating to his followers consumes most of his energy? If he must spend 30 to 50 per cent of his time oiling the organizational wheels to work in harmony —as the author of *Neurotics in the Church* maintains—how can he lead this "machinery" in any meaningful witness in society? It is this custodial care role—this perpetual vigil to keep the boat from rocking—that disillusions many ministers. They feel like a coach who never succeeds in entering his team into competition because he spends all of his time trying to get the members to play together.

The denominational machinery adds to this problem by gearing its many programs to the layman as an individual—

or even as a group—but always as he or they sit in the church building. Everything is tuned to *educating* the layman. Even our social action committees are largely study committees rather than action committees. There is little structure for meeting the world in concentrated action where this world needs to be met. This is probably why the civil rights movement has caught the imagination of many concerned people. Not only is there a cause—there is also a program for corporate action. There is something people can do—not by themselves as individuals, but as a group. They can picket, march, sit-in, suffer—together. But what does the layman do with all of the material with which he is fed by our denominational programs? What takes him beyond studying together to action together in our very complex society? The whole structure of our churches may have to be realigned to activate the Church's witness in a program of constructive action in the world.

The Church Is Losing Ground

The repercussions of this crisis in the ministry take us beyond the local congregation and even the denomination to the Church as a force in the world. Numberwise the Church is losing ground. It has been estimated that by the year 2000, only 20 per cent of the world's population will be Christian as compared to 35 per cent in 1900. But this in itself would be no cause for alarm if the witness of the Church were not also waning. Even in our country there is evidence to indicate that the religious revival is over and even our numbers may begin to decline. Our membership gains in recent years have not kept up with the population increase. The Gallup Poll indicates that there has been a general trend downward in church attendance since 1959. In 1964 it reached the lowest percentage for over a decade—45 per cent as compared to 49 per cent of the adult population in 1955.

The more important question concerns our witness. Our record here is not nearly so good as our numbers. Too often our churches have been mirrors of our culture rather than critics of it. Our members have been more concerned about their vested interests in this world than they have about their commitment to Christ in this world. When this happens the Church loses its witness and fails in its ministry. This failure has been demoralizing to many pastors—also to many laymen. But the pastor has a vocational stake in the Church. He becomes restless when he feels his leadership in witnessing is frustrated. He agonizes over the complacency of his members and the pettiness of their personal antagonisms, and if he sees no way out, his restlessness may become despair.

Spiritual Care of the Pastor Himself

For the sake of others to whom he ministers, the pastor needs to take care of his own spiritual health. But he must also care for his spiritual health for his own sake. If others have needs, so also does he. If the religious problems of others warrant his attention, so also do his own. This is a concern for the laity, too, for they have the responsibility not only to receive care from the pastor, but also to give care to *him*. He is dependent upon them even as they are dependent upon him.

It is more difficult in some ways for a clergyman to preserve his spiritual life than it is for a layman. Because religion is his vocation it can easily become professionalized. He is so identified with it that its professionalization may extend even into his solitude. Where then is the religious person behind the religious professional? I would imagine that a comparable situation could occur with a professional ball player. Playing ball is for enjoyment. But what happens to this enjoyment when playing ball becomes one's work? Is it then any longer play?

When Religion Becomes a Profession

The problem begins in the seminary. Students come to the seminary hoping to find a faith-strengthening atmosphere. To their dismay they discover that their religion becomes academic—the subject of their learning activity. They find it hard, for example, to switch from their use of the Bible as a class assignment to a devotional use for their spiritual sustenance. When God is intellectualized what happens to the divine-human encounter? The same problem occurs with corporate worship. Because the service is a part of their learning experience they easily become critics rather than worshipers. When they realize what is happening, they too can despair. Is God an idea about which I learn—or a person whom I know? So also when religion becomes a profession, what happens to its nonprofessional character?

In spite of what the layman may think, the pastor is not "out of it"—he is not spared their temptations because of his office. In fact, because of his office, these very temptations can be more devious—perhaps because he is supposed to be immune. He partakes of the same distorted atmosphere as others, and his vocation has its own particular susceptibility to the diseases of society. Yet because of the uniqueness of his function, he can have these diseases without the usual symptoms.

Inseparable from the minister's pastoral care of others is his pastoral care of himself. Pastoral care is not a mechanical process that depends on gimmicks or techniques. The Word of God and the Sacraments are indispensable. So also is the *person* of the pastor. The pastoral relationship which is so important in pastoral care is dependent upon the person of the pastor. When his own needs as a person are satisfied, he is able to give love to his people. It is with his person that he maintains his involvement with people, his interest in their interests, and his concern about their lives.

We shall attempt in this book to confront the problem at

hand by holding up the mirror. Since the crisis is really a joint crisis, it is a mirror into which pastor and layman can look together. The pastor's calling is not dependent upon his saintliness. This we shall discover if we were not aware of it before. To some laymen this realization may come as somewhat of a shock. They may be temporarily disillusioned, as adolescents often become with their parents when they discover that ministers are ordinary human beings. The family analogy is even more pertinent since the trend today is toward counseling the family as a group rather than as individuals. The local congregation is the immediate expression of the family of God. Both pastor and layman are children of God—they are priests in their own right before God. The pastor differs from the layman in that he is called by God through the people of God to serve as their leader in the worship and work of the congregation. The word *serve* is well chosen since it means the same as to *minister*. Their problems, therefore, are family problems and should be worked through together.

We Are All in the Same Boat

While the crisis is new, the problem is old. The original ministers were the twelve apostles. As fine as their leadership must have been, the laity were soon grumbling about it. As an expression of their life together the early church had a common treasury into which the "haves" contributed and from which the "have nots" received. But the Hellenists "have nots" felt they were discriminated against in favor of the Palestinian "have nots." The crisis was acute enough for the apostles to take stock of their structure and to decide that it was inadequate for the situation. They asked the laity to choose seven of their number to administer this treasury so that they themselves could concentrate on prayer and the ministry of the Word. It is significant that the tension arose between those of ethnic and cultural differences. The solution proved to be effective but it was reached only after holding up the mirror. (Acts 6:1-6)

Holding up the mirror is no easy task, for the mirror is a threat. What we see may not make us feel good. In fact it may even depress us. Yet, for whatever comfort it may offer, I could not hold up the mirror if I had not looked into it myself. What you see is what I see—what we all see. At times the layman may feel exposed, and at other times, the pastor. But essentially it is the family together sharing in the experience, for we are all partakers in a common humanity. Naturally we are defensive—but we can be defensive together since we are all in the same boat. Besides, what is there to defend? Our heritage is one of trust in the grace of God rather than in our own perfection. A little honest sharing may make us more grateful for this grace, and this in itself is a mark of spiritual health.

The Christian "Ladder Complex"

Grace is the most difficult of all concepts to translate into our personal experience. Most of us are bedeviled with the ladder complex in regard to the Christian life. The ladder is the way to God and the rungs are steps in the process. Grace is the reward we receive for our progress up the ladder. Perhaps our problem is that not enough of us have been on relief. Most of us have what we have because we have worked for it. Also we are further removed from the Depression of the thirties in which all classes of people were united in poverty by that great leveler. In fact, some of the financial caution of older members—an irritation to some younger pastors —can be traced to this devastating era. Yet, grace is not our right—our due. We cannot expect it as such or demand it— as some who have grown up on relief may do. Otherwise it is no longer grace but our rightful dole. So receiving relief in itself is no guarantee that one can understand grace. For this understanding, he needs more than bankruptcy: he needs also the conviction that he deserves nothing—in religious language that he is damned, and justly so. Then his attitude toward the help that comes at this point—and it is only at this point that it comes—is that it is in truth, *grace*.

When the biblical writer said that he was chief of sinners, he was not necessarily indulging in false modesty. This could have been his honest evaluation of himself after he had looked in the mirror—and probably was. A person who disparages a compliment may not simply be trying to appear humble. He may honestly realize that the compliment does not correspond to all the facts. He knows what the complimenter does not know—namely, the whole story. We see what others cannot see when we look in the mirror—our inner self—our feelings, our motivations, our attitudes, and the opportunities that we have had. If others could see what we see, they might agree with our rejection of the compliment. This is why God's love is God's grace. He sees into our mirror and loves us regardless. Perhaps this is why some laymen find it hard to love their pastor. They want instead to admire him—as though he *had* no mirror. They find it hard to love a sinner.

II. PROBLEMS IN THE RESIDENTIAL PARISH

"It takes guts to be a parish minister!" The speaker was a graduate theological student. "I suppose one of the reasons I'm doing graduate work is that I'm trying to avoid it."

"Can you put into words what it is specifically that you are trying to avoid?" I asked.

"I just don't know whether I could take it," he said. "It seems to me that the activities of the residential parish are far removed from what the Church is supposed to be doing."

If this young fellow were speaking only for himself we could dismiss his feelings. But he speaks for a frightening number of younger clergy. What is this residential parish to which he referred and what is the problem concerning it?

The answer to both of these questions lies in what has been described as "our most segregated hour"—the hour of corporate worship. Segregation from its beginnings in this country has been supported, as it is now, by the churches. We think of this segregation as racial and largely it is. Integrated congregations are increasing but are still few and far between and those that exist have largely token integration —a few whites in a predominately Negro congregation or a few Negroes in a predominately white congregation. It can be argued that this is but a reflection of our segregated neighborhoods. Yet, the reverse is also true. Many a white church is "holding the line" against integration in predominately Negro neighborhoods.

The segregation, however, is also along socioeconomic lines. Those who are accused of being the discriminators are uncomplimentarily referred to as *wasps*—white Anglo-Saxon Protestants. These are the people who, having been a part of our culture for a long time, seem to be the most secure in their status. Often overlooked is that the people of Appalachia are also wasps and are high on the priority list for the government's antipoverty help. When some of these wasps move out of their "mountainous ghetto" into our more prosperous areas, they also may not be welcome in some of the wasp churches. When racial integration occurs, it is more likely to be among people with a similar socioeconomic standing. When we refer to the residential parish we are referring to the white middle- and upper middle-class churches of Protestant denominations—including the holiness groups which have "come of age"—in both urban and rural areas.

The problems of these churches and their pastors differ from those of Negro churches and Negro pastors. One group is trying to maintain the *status quo* and the other is striving for change. The Negro pastor is involved in a crusade, while the white congregation is likely to be resisting this crusade. The Negro church building is the center for the dynamic civil rights movement, and the buildings of white churches are centers for holding action. "I believe Negroes should have their rights, but I think they are going at things too fast. Why should they be in with us? Let the Negroes have their own churches." One is struck by the curious use of the word *let*. As Negroes obtain their civil rights and ascend the socioeconomic ladder they risk the danger of becoming like their white counterparts. The Negro pastor may then begin to feel something of the frustration that his white brother is now experiencing.

The Negro pastor also has his problems. Chief among them is his low salary—some conferences having as low as $2500 minimum salaries. This makes recruitment difficult and dampens parental encouragement. The Negro pastor, like the white pastor, is stymied with administrative details so that he, too, longs for a break in the pace and for more of an adventure in self-fulfillment. In spite of the civil rights cause the layman can also frustrate him, for some Negroes do not consciously connect civil rights with the kingdom of God, and others do not distinguish between them. Also, in spite of the fact that many leaders in the civil rights movement are ministers, some Negro ministers are restrained in their participation for the very natural reason that integration in the churches is actually a threat to their present position as pastors of *Negro* churches.

The Class-conscious Church

The problem of the residential parish is a problem that the white churches have asked for. In the rapidly expanding urban centers the Protestant churches have in the main fled the changing neighborhoods of the city for the safety of the suburbs. Here the energetic middle class has been able to preserve its identity. Our churches have cashed in on this identity. The energetic organization of the junior executive and successful salesman characterizes their lay leadership and parish activity. The congregations are the gathering of those with similar social status. This class church, like the class society that it mirrors, is proud of its progress.

The white churches in the rural North are as segregated as the white churches of the rural South. Their class consciousness is of a different character than the urban churches but is of the same essence. In the South, Negroes are in the rural as well as urban areas, while in the North the Negro is largely a city dweller. This leaves large sections of the rural North, particularly of the agricultural Midwest, without any race problem—at least this is the complacent illusion that these churches like to entertain. But the spirit of discrimination is just as strong as in any church that is faced with the problem. In fact, some of them *are* faced with it. While in North Dakota for a church conference, I was seated with a few of the lay delegates in a restaurant when the subject of the race crisis in the South came up. "I can't understand what's wrong with those people that they don't let the Negro have his rights," said one of them. "Maybe it's something like the way we treat the Indians here in North Dakota," said another. "There's no comparison," said the first man rather indignantly. "Negroes—well, they're people —they have initiative. Indians are just plain worthless. You can't treat them any differently."

However, most of these rural and small-town churches are happy that they have no interracial challenge. They are satisfied to let the larger metropolises bear all the responsibility. Most of these communities have made no gesture to the Negro that would make him feel welcome. The fact is that he is not welcome. I am personally acquainted with a city of 70,000 people with a Negro population of seventy-five. For years one of the leading industries of this city refused to hire Negroes because of the fear that other Negroes would move into the community as a result and the community would blame the industry. The dominant sentiment of the community seems to be a hope that the lopsided proportion will stay the way it is. The fear of the Negro "moving in" would be just as great were it a live possibility as it is on the other side of the "wall" in the metropolis.

The question that haunts the residential parishes of city, town, and country is the one from the Bible, "And who is my neighbor?" Jesus answered this question with the parable of the good Samaritan. He did more than describe what being neighborly means; he struck hard at the ethnic prejudice of his audience. The Samaritan was looked down upon by the Jews. Were Jesus addressing our residential parishes, the counterpart to the Samaritan would be the Negro. It must have been hard for those Jews to have listened to this story of a *good* Samaritan with whom a Jewish Levite and a Jewish priest were unfavorably compared. When Jesus had finished the story and asked his questioners, "Which of these three do you think proved neighbor to the man who fell among the robbers?" one of them answered significantly, "The one who showed mercy on him." He could not bring himself to say "the Samaritan."

Love in the residential parish tends to be discriminating rather than overflowing. "They're not our kind of people—they're better off by themselves. Besides, what would the neighbors think!" I have a former student who is pastor of a residential parish in a changing neighborhood. He organized a teen-age club from the community. I was with him on one occasion and met the members of his club. They were largely Negroes and Puerto Ricans. Soon critics in the congregation were referring to them as "hoodlums." After ten months the congregation voted to lock the church's doors to the club. The reason given—church property was endangered and meetings were creating a neighborhood nuisance. The young pastor held his ground. Much of the opposition, he said, was attributable to racial bigotry. His idea for the program was "to help the kids in the community, to infiltrate the love of Christ and to show the church really cares."[1] When he was asked by the press if he planned to resign he said that he felt the congregation's action was an indication of how much they needed his ministry and that he would stay. "It takes guts to be a parish minister." Many would have resigned.

This discriminating "love" is so much a part of middle-class thinking that politicians who represent this class may assume it as right and reasonable. In a recent election campaign a candidate for re-election to Congress was attacked by his opponent for his voting record. He had consistently voted against measures that would have helped poorer sections of the country. He defended himself by saying that the district that he represented was a prosperous district and the measures he voted against would benefit only poorer districts. He must have felt that this sort of discrimination would appeal to his constituency. How far removed seem the words of St. Paul, "I do not mean that others should be

eased and you burdened, but that as a matter of equality
your abundance at the present time should supply their
want, so that their abundance might supply your want, that
there may be equality. As it is written, 'He who gathered
much had nothing over, and he who gathered little had no
lack.'" (II Cor. 8:13-15)

Fear of the "Have Nots"

The concern of the "haves" seems to be that the "have
nots" will take advantage of them. Regardless of how we
may justify this concern on the basis of the value system of
our culture, the fact remains that it is not a Christian concern. We hate to see anybody get the best of us, but we do
not mind it nearly so much if we get the best of them. Our
delight is to get more back than we put out. We carry this
obsession even into our dealings with God. We try in one
way or another to work out a bargain with Him, so that
much to our delight we get the better of the deal. In his
Works of Love, Søren Kierkegaard sees in this attitude the
antithesis to the Christian spirit. The concern of the Christian is that he *gives*. True, he may be taken advantage of!
In the eyes of the world his action may seem foolish. "The
sons of this world are wiser in their own generation than the
sons of light." (Luke 16:8) But the vision of the sons of light
is not limited to the value system of this world. Their vision
extends into eternity. "Love is just as well aware as anyone
of everything which mistrust knows," says Kierkegaard, "yet
without being mistrustful."[2] In giving, the Christian cannot
lose—he can only be disappointed. For love's sake a Christian may refuse to give. But the anger with which we refuse
betrays our spirit.

The residential parish in city, town, and country tends to
be the church of the self-made man. "Let the others work
for it," he says, "like I had to do. I didn't get anything for
nothing! Why should they?" Again, how far distant sound

the words of St. Paul: "Who maketh thee to differ from another? And what hast thou that thou didst not receive? Now if thou didst receive it, why dost thou glory, as if thou hadst not received it?" (I Cor. 4:7) No wonder justification by grace is difficult to realize if we insist on this kind of self-justification. It is part of the warp and woof of a competitive society. As someone has observed, "The business of America is business." One gets his worth by working for it. The reward for his work is success. With success comes the accumulation of property. Property rights, then, become sacred rights and the protection of property has precedence over almost everything else. The teen-age club for example, had to go because church *property* was endangered. In Washington, D.C., there is a pioneer inner-city ministry called Community of Christ. In differentiation from a parish, the Community has no orientation to a building. Instead of seeking its own property, the group simply rents its quarters. "We want to feel free to move with any urban renewal shift," said the pastor, "but of more importance is our realization that owning property has made the Church not only in the world, but *of* the world. We want to avoid this potential for corruption."

The prevalent attitude toward worth and accomplishment has helped to make America what it is. But it has been hard on the Christianity of the Church. Not only does it cause difficulties with justification by grace, but it is becoming increasingly out of tune with our changing culture. A large bakery, for example, that once hired hundreds of people can now be operated twenty-four hours a day, seven days a week, by seven people as a result of cybernation. Even the work of the seven consists largely in button pushing. Automation is daily depleting the number of jobs available for an exploding population. Addressing a large gathering of Christian youth, labor leader Walter Reuther challenged the churches to help labor with the growing problem of leisure time. With the four-day work week in sight and the possibility of moonlighting decreasing, we are confronted with the spiritual challenge of having a purpose for living other than working to get money.

Is a New Theology Needed?

We are faced with the necessity of developing a different attitude toward work and vocation. This may mean a change in our theology. Our present doctrine developed from the reformational need to give religious significance to all work. Every person—the servant girl with her pots and pans as well as the clergyman with his prayers—glorifies God in his work. From this wholesome beginning the subtle implication has filtered in that work in itself is a religious obligation that establishes one's worth. Culturally speaking it provides one with the means for self-reliance and independence. It is just a small step from this to the attitude that one's accomplishments through his work are self-congratulatory and a justifiable basis for judging others who have not worked and therefore are not justified. As one layman put it, "Doesn't it say in the Bible that if anyone won't work, he shouldn't eat!" So it does. But the purpose for this work is something different than our own. According to the Bible work provides for self-reliance and this is good. It also keeps us out of mischief. Yet there is an altruistic purpose. "Let the thief no longer steal, but rather let him labor, doing honest work with his hands, so that he may be able to give to those in need." (Eph. 4:28) Actually no change in theology is needed, but rather a return to a biblical theology. The Christian purpose for work is not primarily to accumulate property and a sense of pride, but to be able to give to those in need.

The Christian's growing alignment with the values of the middle class has contributed to a dangerous split with the objectives of organized labor. For example, in my own denomination, when the president of United States Steel,

Roger Blough, spoke at one of our denominational colleges and received an honorary degree, there was no appreciable negative reaction. But when Walter Reuther spoke to our youth convention, there was a loud hue and cry. Not that the labor union consists of the *have nots*—far from it. But it expresses the *sentiments* of the *have nots*. It is these sentiments that our residential churches often find repugnant.

The rural church has traditionally been strong on self-reliance and suspicious of unions. The union was a city invention. With the rise of the National Farmers' Organization with its violent holding action, however, the farmer is faced with his own union problems. On the right is the conservative Farm Bureau—more or less the spokesmen for the *haves*. In the middle is the Farmers Union. On the left is the National Farmers Organization, which expresses the sentiments of the *have nots*. Can those who ally themselves with one or the other of these groups find fellowship together in the same local congregation? Can the rural church succeed where the urban church has failed and give priority to the Christian witness regardless of how it judges this or that force in society?

Our challenge as Christians is to involve the Church in the various forces of society rather than bringing these alignments into the Church. If we put less energy into trying to perpetuate a romantic notion about the spirituality of all work and faced instead the dehumanizing elements in many jobs, we could put more energy into encouraging one another to bear the Christian witness in the union, in management, in business, and in the professions.

The Reformation Was Sparked by a Building Program

When the merits of work center in the accumulation of property, the Church's interest will also shift to property. We have witnessed a phenomenal church-building program in the last decades. Most residential parishes during this time have either relocated entirely or have erected new sanctuaries, or new educational units or new parish houses or expansions of the same. These buildings have been built with functional designs for financial reasons and also because the buildings are an expression of the energetic program that is carried on in them. While it is true that a church building is used less than most other buildings, it nevertheless is an expression of the activity of the congregation because it is the locus of this activity. Consequently the great emphasis in this church program is to "get the crowd out"—that is, to get the crowd into the building. In all of these activities care must be taken not to offend people because they are needed to pay off the debt.

Thus the residential parish has become another vested interest in the societal picture rather than the leaven in all society. Ominously we recall that the Reformation had its catalyst in a church-building program. The sale of indulgences which provoked Luther's protest was to provide money to build St. Peter's Church in Rome. Perhaps our current building-centered program will catalyze another much needed reformation. And the discontent of many clergymen as well as laymen indicates that it may already have begun.

Pastor or Club Manager?

In his darker moments the minister may feel that the structure of the residential parish limits rather than channels the Christian witness. It seems that his is a maintenance ministry—a ministry of keeping things going—and there is nothing very exciting about it. In the Kansas City area there is a Country Club Christian Church. The name comes from the name of the district. Yet, the minister may feel at times that his church is more of a social organization than a witnessing fellowship. It may not be up to country-club standards—it may even be a family affair as in some rural congregations—but it is a club nevertheless. As one pastor said in a despairing mood, "What am I accomplishing really? I am keeping it going—and going well, I guess—but why? And what for?"

Walter Wagoner warns that this restlessness of the younger clergy about the cultural conditioning of the Church and the established forms of parish structure can no longer be disregarded. Otherwise we may expect a maverick revolt against the established order. Perhaps this would be a good thing. Perhaps this is the way God intends to work His ways. Our purpose, however, is not to invite revolt but to examine the problem in the hope that it can be remedied.

The minister's frustration stems not only from his parish structure, but from the denominational structure which is built around the parish structure. When I was commenting upon the lack of identity that seems to characterize some ministers, a pastor challenged me. "It's not that the minister lacks an understanding of his calling," he said, "but the congregation has a *different* understanding and the parent church body still *another* understanding, and he may feel he cannot carry out his own idea. Sometimes I wish I were financially independent so that I could carry out my function as I see it. Otherwise, one gets to thinking he could do more good in some other field as a layman."

"What do you think the congregation's conception of a minister is?" I asked. He thought a bit and then said, "A good Joe."

"And the parent church body's conception?"

"A promoter," he said.

The Professional Friend

Many would agree with him. In the science-fiction spoof of the future *The Big Ball of Wax*, the leading ecclesiastical denomination is called "Yourchurch." Instead of being titled "Reverend" or "Father," the clergy of Yourchurch are addressed as "Friendly." The founder of Yourchurch is the

Right Friendly Harry Wilker Murray, who, as one might suspect, had previously been a top merchandising man. In a critical assessment of the minister in *The National Observer,* the Reverend Ernest Werner says that the minister is forced by society to be friendly, which is an agreeable replacement for the ancient pastoral duties. He is then a professional friend, on call at all times.

"You missed your calling, Reverend. You should have been in business. I tell you, you would have made a million!" Something akin to these words is termed in ministerial humor as the layman's highest compliment. To his laymen, he has demonstrated the ability that would have made him a top merchandising man. He is a first-class promoter. Unfortunately, we ministers like this compliment. We feel we have arrived—earned the layman's respect. It is like being called a real man. Being a promoter and being friendly are the two sides of a successful businessman. The only trouble, of course, is that, judged by the same standards of operation, God is a poor businessman.

Besides being a drain on his energies, the pastor's role as a professional friend interferes with his prophetic function, which will not always be interpreted as friendly. "Prophecy," says writer Werner, "is never a member of the Establishment."[3] The promoter can scarcely be a prophet, either, for that which is promoted must acquire popular appeal.

Change always threatens the Establishment. The organized church may not be willing to lose its life even though it means finding it. Things can get too organized—too settled, even too efficient—so that there is no longer any frontier. The younger clergy especially are asking for a frontier. They are questioning the existing order. Is it more culturally conditioned than Christian? And has it now become even *culturally* anachronistic?

In contrast to the parish ministry, the specialized ministries are receiving renewed interest. The lure of the inner-city ministry offers these restless clergymen a frontier. New structures for ministry such as the East Harlem Protestant Parish and the West Side Parish in Chicago are catching the imagination. The ministries of George Webber of the East Harlem Parish and of Don Benedict of the Chicago Social Mission are gaining wide recognition. Inner-city ministries are structureless so far as the past is concerned. The community is mission territory and the parish life is a community life. Old value systems may become irrelevant. The Christian witness may be in a picket line more than in the pulpit and community organization may be more pressing than church organization. Says George Webber, "The present predicament of the church demands that most of these groups (men's fellowship, women's society, missionary group and all the rest) be given up for the sake of mission."[4]

The institutional chaplaincy is another specialized ministry that lures the parish minister. Here he can concentrate on the incapacitated. The chaplaincy is a crisis ministry to people who are open for change. Gone is the clutter of inconsequential formality. Chaplains of mental hospitals and penal institutions often see in their "congregations" more honesty and genuine Christianity than they see in the congregations on the outside. The chaplain's goals are more clearly defined—and more oriented to persons rather than programs. He is concerned with rehabilitating those who are in obvious straits—physically, emotionally, and socially. When he succeeds the results are most gratifying. The self-made man is, happily, not among his parishioners. Rather he sees God's power "made perfect in weakness." Also—and this is not to be overlooked in terms of family life—his evenings are largely free.

Other specializations attractive to the minister are teaching and counseling. Students who leave seminary for graduate school rather than the parish usually hope to teach, either in a college or a seminary. Religion is still the most popular subject for the theologically oriented teacher, but psychology, philosophy, and sociology are also attractive.

Others seek special training to qualify as counselors either on campuses or in church-oriented clinics or even as ministers of counseling in a parish with a team ministry. These specializations also allow for more regular hours and add to one's status as an authority. The advanced academic degree provides additional prestige, which unfortunately the B.D. seems to lack—even though it requires at least three and often four years of education beyond the A.B. degree—obviously more than the M.A.

When the parish minister begins to reflect upon his ministry, he often seriously questions whether he should not consider getting more schooling—or other training—so that he can get involved in some specialized ministry. This is a day of specialization. The general practitioner in medicine may have similar concerns. This trend in itself might be enough to cause the clergyman "general practitioner" to feel restless. The greater problem, however, is that he so often feels his congregation is working against him rather than with him in witnessing to the world. When this resistance is overt and declared, he is engaged in a power struggle with the very people he is supposed to lead.

The inactive list is depressing to any minister. But there are times when he wishes it were larger, providing he could name the additions. These would be the lay leaders who actively resist him. Often they conceal their resistance under the guise of advising caution. But like the yellow caution light, the word means the same as "better not do it" and stops "traffic" as well as the red light. Others offer him passive resistance. They are the apathetic and indifferent. Like a father who complains about his children, the "shepherd" complains about his "flock." They just don't do what they should! At times like these he can empathize with the prophet Elijah, who, after he had tried desperately to witness to Israel and had failed, sat down in defeat under a juniper tree and complained, "It is enough; now, O Lord, take away my life; I am no better than my fathers." (I Kings

19:4) What God told Elijah also applies to the discouraged pastor—"Yet I will leave seven thousand in Israel, all the knees that have not bowed to Baal"—in other words, you are not the only one.

The Layman Can Help

The antidote to the minister's despair is his involvement in the lives of his people. The pastoral aspect of the ministry provides the depth that sustains his morale during the apparent meaninglessness of congregational activities. People in the midst of personal and family crises are open to his ministry. As he gives of himself to these sufferers, he himself experiences a real sense of ministry. The desperation in the crisis pulls down the façades. People are genuine when they are in pain—physical or mental. The things that seemed so important previously are pushed to the side. It is much easier then to distinguish the more important from the less important. What is expressed is honest and personal. As the pastor becomes involved at this level of need, he establishes a relationship that endures. The ties of gratitude and accomplishment are not always associated with obvious success but with being present when one's presence was needed.

There are times when the minister gets fed up with being an administrator. What administrator does not? At these times he may feel justified in asking, "What's it all for?" Administration wears him out but may not provide him with a sense of self-fulfillment. Most congregational activities and projects have their value, but this value might also be questioned. Not so with his pastoral work. The dimensions of relating are all too real for questioning. The very feelings involved testify to the essential nature of the ministry. People are rarely the same following a crisis. The minister's presence may make the difference concerning the quality of the change.

The layman can help the pastor to become involved in the

lives of people. The pastor appreciates it when those in need call upon him rather than letting him discover their plight in some indirect way. Those who are aware of people who are in a crisis should refer them to the pastor—or even better, bring them to him. As the laymen help to make the pastoral ministry available, they are not only helping those in need but are helping the minister to devote his time to that which is of ultimate importance—and therefore inwardly satisfying.

But pastoral care is not confined to the ministry. Every layman is a potential lay pastor. Laymen can reach people who would shy away from a pastor. The scope of a congregation's ministry is enlarged when the layman as well as the minister takes a personal interest in people who have needs. The minister is not the only doer, but the one who leads the congregation in doing. In the mind of St. Paul he is the one who equips the others for their task. "And his gifts were that some should be apostles, some prophets, some evangelists, some pastors and teachers, for the equipment of the saints, for the work of ministry, for the building up of the body of Christ." (Eph. 4:11–12)

III. THE NEED TO SUCCEED

"The business of America is business." The minister not only fights the business invasion of the Church, he is also taken in by it. This is seen most clearly in his need to succeed. The need to succeed has its wholesome side. We are creative by nature and achieving our goals brings a genuine sense of satisfaction. But this need can also be unwholesome when it becomes contaminated by the compulsion to excel that characterizes our competitive society.

The Clerical Status Pyramid

The profession of the ministry is influenced by our age more than most of us would like to think. The following scene could be enacted in almost any ministerial conference. One of the ministers is leaving the conference to become an executive secretary in a department of his church headquarters—another example of specialization that detracts from the parish ministry. The brethren and their wives are having a final get-together with the departing couple, and the spokesman for the group offers these words of farewell: "We are sorry to see you leave. We have enjoyed having you in our midst. But we rejoice that you have been promoted to a greater area of responsibility."

The pastor also is interested in promotion. These words of farewell indicate the direction of this promotion, and it is obviously a downgrading of the parish ministry. This is in line with the demotion of the general practitioner in our age of specialization. He is an authority on nothing. "I'm just a housewife," now has its clergy counterpart in, "I'm just an ordinary parish pastor."

But there is a status structure also *within* the parish ministry. The type of church he has is a rating scale for evaluating the pastor's status. At the bottom of the ladder is the pastor of a small rural parish—or parishes—and at the top is the pastor of a large metropolitan church with a staff that includes one, two, or even three clergy assistants or associates. How many people one has "under him" is a status gauge in the work-a-day world. As one ascends the hierarchical steps to the top, the direction is ominously away from personal involvement with people. The head pastor is usually the administrator. He is also the preacher. He is rarely the pastor. I know of one situation where the head pastor turned over the administrative function to his younger associate in order to concentrate himself on the pastoral and calling ministries. But this is the exception rather than the trend.

The same is true with the specialized ministries. The bishop or his equivalent is increasingly an administrator rather than a pastor. The denominational executive is obviously an administrator. Even the chaplain eyes the status of a chaplain-supervisor in which he can concentrate on teaching student chaplains rather than in calling on patients himself. The college and seminary teacher likes a comparatively low number of teaching hours so that he can give more time to research, writing, and lecturing—all of which tend to remove him from the actual classroom and the student-professor dialogue. Anyone familiar with the elite institutions of higher learning knows the truth of Sydney Harris' definition of a "successful professor" as "not one who has the great influence on his students, but one who has the least contact with them—who works for the glory of the college and for his own fame, while the students are exposed to third-rate teachers."[1]

The Diseases of Industry

Since our church structure is similar to that of the economic world, we can expect our problems to be similar. We suffer from the diseases of industry. Every project must expand to keep the stockholders happy. Even our home mission policies have been based on the principle that every dollar sent out should come back. Naturally this has moved us to concentrate on suburban missions. From the local church council to the denominational administration, the principles of sound investment often predominate. How will it profit us? How will it show a profit? As one wag has put it, we have gone from the *prophet* motive to the *profit* motive. The danger of an institutionalized Christianity is that it is just that—an institution in society which does not see the Christian life apart from cooperation and involvement within the projects of the institution. The locus of the Church is in society—not as one institution among others, but as the conscience—the leaven—of society. The Church's "program" is in the secular world and not in withdrawal from it.

Even his emotional problems are more similar to those of the businessman than the pastor would like to admit. But the businessman *can* admit them. He can be open about the fact that he is interested in advancement. But the minister makes such an admission defensively if at all. "I am already forty-three years old," he says. "My next congregation will be a very important move in my career. I have three children who will be going to college soon. I've got to think of these things even though I hate to."

He "hates to" because he is supposed to be interested in "spiritual" things. When he has conflicts over his "worldly" concerns, he may try to solve them by effacing himself in one way or another to show he is humble. Like other leaders, the minister wants to be liked by his people. He may not go to the extreme of Willy Loman in being "well-liked" but he can understand Willy Loman.[2] Pastors are often evaluated by how the congregation "takes" to them. "They like him," we say, or "some like him and some don't," or "the majority seem to wish he would move." Some pastors even face an annual vote to determine whether the congregation "likes" him well enough to retain his services for another year. The critical innuendos that some ministers let fall concerning their predecessors—poor records, lax pastoral practice, personal favoritism, and the like—are usually precipitated by the pressure they feel from the congregation to match this predecessor's popularity.

The pressure to conform can put a damper on the minister's witness.

Explaining his reasons for desiring to return to school, a former parish pastor said, "I was trying to reach out with my ministry into the community, but I was criticized for spending too much time with those who were outside the congregation."

"Why should that have stopped you?" I asked.

"I had never thought of it in that way," he said.

His answer indicates how deeply ingrained even in the ministry is the other-directed trait of our culture. The authority by virtue of his authoritative role has a lonely path—a path made lonely by the fact that he knows his own mind.

The Emphasis on Becoming Rather Than Being

Ours is a highly competitive society for men—and the minister is, with few exceptions, male. The man establishes his worth by excelling in his vocation. This is why the promotion means so much. His milieu is hostile and the casualties are many. Alongside this competitive value system of success by achievement, the Christian concepts of worth through grace and of walking by faith and not by sight seem highly abstract.

President Lyndon B. Johnson is an example of the successful man. Rising from the modest position of an elementary schoolteacher to the Presidency of the United States, Lyndon Johnson is known as a compulsive worker. His success story is more than an accident. Early in his life his father would rout him out of bed by saying, "Get up, Lyndon, get up! Everybody in town has an hour's start on you already."[3] Life is a race and already some have a head start. The anxiety is sown—somebody may get ahead of you if you don't get up and get at it.

His predecessor in the highest office of the land, John F. Kennedy, was also an example of a successful man. Again the story concerns a father who impressed upon his children that life is a race and instilled in them the drive to win. Said President Kennedy's sister Eunice, "Even when we were six and seven years old, Daddy always entered us in public swimming races. . . . The thing he always kept telling us was that coming in second was just no good. The important thing was to win—don't come in second or third—that doesn't count—but win, win, win."[4] When young John was lagging in his progress at preparatory school, his father wrote him, "Now Jack, I don't want to give the impression that I am a nagger, for goodness knows I think that is the worst thing any parent can be. After long experience in sizing up people, I definitely know you have the goods and you can go a long way. Now aren't you foolish not to get all there is out of what God has given you?"[5] We can also see the results of this pressure in the lives of the late President's brothers, Robert and Edward.

Ironically, the type of parental pressure exerted upon Johnson and the Kennedys is warned against by some child psychologists. It creates tensions, they say, that make the child feel that he is unacceptable unless he is achieving—or better, excelling. The emphasis is on *becoming* rather than *being*—on getting ahead rather than on enjoying the game. Yet the approach evidently works! At least it would be difficult to account for Lyndon Johnson or any of the Kennedys without it. It is likely also that many of our successful ministers can give credit to a strong parent who instilled in them the drive to succeed.

In apparent contrast to this drive are the words of Jesus,

"But many that are first will be last and the last first." (Mark 10:31) What do these words mean? We often explain them by saying that some obscure old lady in scant circumstances may be doing more in God's eyes than the bishop of her diocese. But this application takes the issue outside of our competitive system. Men do not compete with little old ladies—they compete with their own peers. What about a man in his early forties who seems to be getting nowhere as far as his vocation is concerned? Could he possibly be considered first—in contrast to the go-getter in the same vocation who is headed toward the top? At this point Jesus' words can be frightening. Is it possible that the goals toward which we devote our lives are selling us short—that we are living an illusion? As Christians we pay lip service to a possible reversal of cultural values, but gear our goals to the value system that seems to work in our society. We do the same with our children. We want them to acknowledge the reversal of values, but to fit into the system.

The Ministerial Pole Vaulters

How do we evaluate our worth? We have already mentioned prestige in terms of bigness—big church, big staff, big popularity, big authority. But there is another *big* that usually accompanies these—the big salary. Ministers' salaries in comparison to those of other professionals are low. But within the profession itself there is a large variance. Salaries are symbols of worth as much as means of livelihood. The pastor knows he is not worth what the physician is. So he compares his salary with that of other clergymen. And here is where the tension comes in. The main trouble with ministers' salaries, says Walter Wagoner, is not that they are low, but that they are not regularized. In other words they are competitive. There are no orderly systems of advancement. Even those churches with episcopal controls have difficulty bucking the politicking of popularity.

Using athletic figures, artist James Crane pictures the Jesuit ministry with its chain of command as a pyramid in which each person is related to the other in a structure. In contrast he pictures the Protestant ministry as a pole vaulting contest. Each man as an individual rises into the air from the sheer force of his own leap. The Jesuit system would compare to the railroad unions with their strict adherence to the seniority system for advancement or to the United States Congress, which has the same system for its positions of power and influence. The Protestant ministry, on the other hand, compares more validly to management, where a younger man can pole vault over the heads of veterans if he has "more on the ball" or better connections or is "well liked" by the right people. With the leap comes the leap in salary, not because he needs more money, but because it is the symbol of the leap. In a *Time* magazine survey of the financial picture of ministers, Dr. Merle E. Fish, Jr., president of the Church Federation of Los Angeles, is quoted as saying, "Most of the fellows I know who are underpaid are incompetent. They couldn't make it any better anywhere else." Vice President Magee Wilkes of Southern California School of Theology agrees. "The best men make the most money. Churches are willing to pay for leadership."[6] This view of the salary places the minister in the bind of being labeled a mediocre minister if his salary is not competitively high.

This competitive aspect of the Protestant ministry has its wholesome and unwholesome sides. Competition usually heightens production. Without it businesses as well as churches tend to become complacent. When a new family moves into a neighborhood they may have as many as three ministers call on them. One man told me that he and his family had only been in their new home fifteen minutes before the most aggressive of the community ministers was ringing their door bell. Similarly they will be called upon by several dairies and the one arriving first may get their milk order. The go-getters prosper in competition. Those with less drive do not. In fact, the very competitive atmosphere may deter what abilities they have.

The competitive world is a hostile world. It shows no mercy to those who cannot qualify. The survival is that of the fittest. This hostile world where the man's self is spent cuts into his fellowship with other men. For the minister this begins in the seminary, for here, too, there is competition. The student is graded on a comparative basis known as the curve. His desire to get ahead causes him involuntarily to hope his competitors do not do as well. He knows he should rejoice in the good grades of his fellow students, but he finds it hard when these make his own grades appear less good. So the tense and competitive question resounds in the halls of the seminary when the test papers are returned—"What'd you get?"

I experienced this same tension at a Spiritual Life Mission conducted by the churches of a community. Each morning the pastors and missioners met to receive stimulation and to compare notes. As we gathered, the same question could be heard. "How many? How many did you have out last night?" To make matters worse, each evening's attendance figures were tabulated numberwise, percentagewise, and offeringwise, for each congregation for comparison. Life is a race and the pressure is on to come out on top!

The pressure is on—and it is hard on the spirit! Should he stay in his present parish or should he move? Should he request another assignment—put his name in for a call? In seminary he was told that such things were under the direction of the Holy Spirit. After he has been in the ministry for a while he may wonder. Can the Holy Spirit be operating through the politics of church officialdom—particularly when the politics have been unfavorable to him? What determines whether this or that minister is called to such and such a church? Is it the Holy Spirit or chance breaks or freak circumstances or administrative preference? Or does the Holy Spirit actually operate through such procedures?

These questions grow more pressing as the minister grows older. The Church is harder on the older man than is industry. When a certain desirable parish was in the process of calling a minister, a neighboring pastor was asked if he thought he was being considered. "Not a chance," he said. "They're looking for someone between the ages of thirty-four and thirty-five." The speaker happened to be in his forties. More than in any other profession, experience is devalued in the ministry. Youth and advanced academic degrees are more important. The congregation's desire for a "younger man" is explained by saying, "We need somebody with a lot of drive who will be good with young people." The implication is that such a person must himself be young. The pastor who has passed into middle life may find himself asking the question against his will—"Is it too late?" And he cannot leave the profession for some other work like the younger man. With the age factor against him, his training is too limited. For him the parish ministry is harder to get out of than it was to enter. As the unlimited future of the seminary graduate becomes more and more limited for the middle-aged pastor, he is faced with the possibility that the success which he has achieved may be the success to which he shall be limited. And this can be quite disillusioning.

The pressure is on—and it is hard on the body. The tensions that weaken the body's organs do not spare the minister. He participates in the same unhealthy vocational pressure that wears away the health of other men. His wife, like other wives, can look forward to five years of widowhood according to the statistics. Because he is oriented toward the "spirit" the minister may neglect his body even more than other men. "Bodily exercise profits little," said St. Paul, and for some ministers it is neglected altogether. Consequently they deprive themselves of the temporary release from tension that such exercise can provide.

Professional Jealousy and Fear of Failure

It is pressures such as these that cause a minister to resent other ministers—to be jealous of those who get the "better" parishes or the coveted administrative offices—and to become disgruntled and critical because of his own failure to ascend the ladder. Usually, however, he does not recognize his resentment as jealousy but as legitimate anger. The whole system seems unjust and he vents his reaction upon the most likely scapegoat—the person who seems to be profiting from the system. As Daniel D. Walker has observed,[7] these disgruntled men feel their true worth has been unrecognized—and maybe it has—and therefore feel forced to say and do things that others whose road to success has been smoother do not feel necessary. This behavior can make him even more unattractive to the ecclesiastical hierarchy, as it would to an industrial hierarchy were he an employee. So the situation can go from bad to worse. Bitterness is a poison. For a minister it is a deadly poison because it destroys the spirit by which he ministers. Disgruntled because of his own failure to "climb the ladder," he directs his energies into shaking the ladder under those who supposedly are ascending it.

The sense of failure is very threatening. Under such pressure to succeed, the pastor's defenses may emerge at any indication of failure. A minister who prided himself on his standards was remonstrating with his fellow pastors at the local ministerium for tolerating members in their congregation who belonged to a certain questionable fraternal order. This was too much for a veteran clergyman who had lived in the community for over twenty years. "You have them in your congregation too," he said. "I most certainly do not," replied the pastor. "All right," said the veteran, beginning to number on his fingers, "I'll name them. First there is—" At this point the pastor interrupted, "Stop!" he demanded. "I won't hear any more of this!" Behind the apparent bluster was a panic-stricken man for whom illusion was preferable to reality.

This fear of failure is one reason why ministers find it difficult to work together in pastoral problems. That one of his own members would consult another minister may seem tantamount to a rejection of *him*. It is almost as though his children had gone to someone else's parents rather than to their own. Instead of recognizing the value of intraprofessional help, he may see it as a judgment upon himself. "Where have I failed?" he asks himself. But to the parishioner he may express only irritation. "Why didn't you come to me in the first place?" Or, "Why are you telling tales out of school?" Such pressures to succeed cause the minister to feel resentful when he is thwarted in his program and discouraged when there is a lack of response to his efforts. He needs encouragement from his laity. Most of us can last just so long without some tangible evidence of appreciation before our spirits begin to drop. His work is more than his "church work"—it is his vocation, not his avocation. Supporting his program—his ministry—is also supporting his morale.

The Congregation Fashions Its Pastor

Because of this interdependence it is hard for a minister to feel neutral toward his congregation. When his feelings are negative, they may soon color his preaching. The people in the pew have more to do with the kind of sermons that they hear than they realize. Any audience influences a speaker. But the consistency of the congregation as audience fashions its own image in the preacher's mind. He prepares his sermons and preaches them under the influence of this image. When this image is threatening or irritating, he tends to attack it. Like the western horse opera, his sermons may center around "good guys" and "bad guys." The "good guys" are those who cooperate with the program of the congregation and the "bad guys" are those who do not. The "good guys" attend church regularly, are willing to teach in the Sunday school or sing in the choir, and contribute to the building fund of the church. The "bad guys" do none of these things.

Good and evil become quite uncomplicated in the thought world of the preacher who is reacting negatively to his congregation. The dynamics of his conflict tend to shorten his perspective from the world in which he and his congregation live to the little world which he and his congregation share. This simplifies things but it also falsifies them. Such preaching leads to a very shallow conception of sin—one that excludes the pastor altogether. He and his family normally do all the things which he accuses the "bad guys" of not doing. One might, of course, refer to a possible difference in motivation, but one does not go into motives. This would complicate things further.

The resistance to face the ambivalences in his own soul may leave the pastor vulnerable to the *hidden* aspects of evil—specifically his own potential to succumb to the very devil he is fighting. This potential is an old theme for the novelists. In Somerset Maugham's *Rain* the missionary who rails against the "sins of the flesh" himself succumbs to the lure of his own unrecognized lust, and before him, Henry Fielding's clergyman Mr. Thwackum in *Tom Jones* is the supporter of the Pharisaical approach to morality.

By the same token, such preaching leads to an equally shallow conception of righteousness. According to it, one is justified by his good works in terms of his involvement in the congregation's program. How justification by grace fits into this system of merit is difficult to ascertain. Pressed to defend themselves theologically, such preachers would probably say that it is because one is justified by faith that he does these works. But since there is little concern given to the motivations for these works, this point is likely to be missed by the hearers.

As a facetious footnote to this discrepancy it could be noted that the preacher has the last word in these matters. He also preaches funeral sermons! If a parishioner has been a "good boy" the preacher is quite likely to mention this in the final eulogy—and most of us would like a good send-off.

It would be difficult to determine whether the pastor or the congregation has the more influence on the other. The best we can say is that each is to some extent the creator of the other. The congregation is not innocent in these foibles of the pastor since his negative involvement with them brings out the worst in him. The irony is that we resent what we help to bring about. So the parishioners get together and criticize the pastor and the local pastors get together and criticize the congregations.

There ought to be opportunities for direct criticism between people and pastor in each congregation. Although it is more difficult to talk to people directly than to talk about them, it is also more Christian. In addition, direct confrontation has a way of ultimately opening our eyes to our own contribution to the situation that is offensive.

The pulpit is a risky place for personal confrontation. Since there is no opportunity for a response, the pastor's advantage may embolden him to scold rather than to confront. The best place for this encounter is in the regular get-togethers of the congregation, around the council table, at the board meetings, or in the homes of the members. Here within the fellowship there is opportunity for an exchange of ideas. The confrontation can be initiated by the layman as well as the pastor. There may be some anxious moments when this happens and this is why we hesitate. But the opportunity for resolving the tension is much greater when it is brought out into the open within the fellowship—within the body—where we are all members one of another.

IV. THE PASTOR'S PERSONALITY PROBLEMS

In concentrating on one profession, we may give the impression that other professions are untroubled. Such, of course, is far from the truth. Even psychologists do not escape the judgment. Tests at the Illinois Institute of Technology comparing psychologists with businessmen revealed that psychologists worried more about money and as much about their jobs and marital difficulties. What made it worse for the psychologists is that the tests also showed that people who are frank, open, and sincere have fewer fears. But ministers are also part of the human family and are not exempt from human problems.

What sort of a person goes into the ministry? Naturally, it would be unwise to generalize at this point. Laymen do this often enough as it is. Paul W. Tibbetts, Jr., the pilot whose plane dropped the first atomic bomb over Hiroshima, was described in a newspaper account as "a slight, austere man who looks more like a minister than a soldier."[1] Even my own teen-age son, when informed that a certain visitor to our house was a minister, said, "He sure doesn't look like a minister!" Yet the nature of the work would tend to draw those with specific interests. Being a religious person, the minister tends to be conscientious—concerned about values—about self-improvement. His emphasis is on *becoming*—on changing—on converting. If the present ministerial crisis were aggravated by his own personality problems, we would expect that such problems would reflect these predispositions. Being concerned about the improvement of the human situation can become distorted so that one becomes a perfectionist. Since the ministry centers in relationships,

the minister with perfectionist tendencies may become unrealistic in his demands upon himself and upon his people.

The Dangers of Perfectionism

The normal demands upon a minister are heavy enough
without being compounded by problems in his personality.
Perfectionist tendencies create havoc in the ministry. The
task is so comprehensive that it is in a continual state of
incompleteness and imperfection—and this can be agonizing to the conscientious person. But what is wrong with
desiring perfection? Jesus Himself said, "You, therefore,
must be perfect, as your Heavenly Father is perfect." (Matt.
5:48) St. Paul also challenges the minister to "present every
man perfect in Christ Jesus." (Col. 1:28) There is a difference, however, in setting one's goals at perfection and being
a perfectionist. Setting our goals at perfection grows out of
our sense of self-worth, while perfectionism is an attempt
to establish our worth.

In setting his goal at perfection, the minister is hoping
to come as close to it as possible. This does not mean he
must punish himself for not reaching it. Our justification as
Christians is based on something other than our achieve-
ments. The perfectionist likewise sets his goal at perfection,
but for a different reason. He needs to be perfect in order
to accept himself. Since he naturally falls short of his goal,
he is continually punishing himself for being a failure.

The perfectionist is overcompensating for his extreme
sense of inferiority. Since his doubts about his worth are so
strong, only perfection can reassure him. Being very sensitive about his deficiencies, he may become quite defensive
if others should allude to them. Perfectionists tend to run
themselves down, but they do not expect others to agree
with them. In fact, it may irritate them if they do. One of
the reasons we run ourselves down is that we hope thereby
to move others to build us up. The perfectionist is seeking

reassurance. Yet verbal reassurance gives only temporary relief. The real goal—perfection itself—forever eludes him. Even if he should attain it, it is doubtful if he could accept it. The perfectionist is a guilty person, and he is driven by this guilt to punish himself. Not all perfectionists are in the ministry; some are in the pew. They ought to understand each other.

Perfectionism is stimulated by the projects in which congregational life abounds. Some of these are inspired by church headquarters. Others are indigenous to the activism of the parish itself. Every project has its goal and every goal engenders its own anxiety. "Will we make it?" "How did you make out?" Symbolic of this *projectitis* is the familiar thermometer poster on the inside wall of the parish house— although I have occasionally seen them on the back wall of the sanctuary or on an improvised billboard on the church lawn. The brilliant red of the mercury rises with each new achievement toward the goal which is printed in large letters—or figures—at the top of the thermometer.

With "thermometers" in all directions, the pastor can develop anxiety over each. Like Martha in the New Testament he becomes encumbered with many things—many "spiritual" goals, and the anxiety he develops over each is indicative that it is not the one thing needful which Jesus recommended to Martha. If the failure to meet a goal is tantamount to a personal failure, his identity as a person actually includes the projects. Here then is the source of his anxiety. The perfectionist needs the projects as much as the projects need him. He cannot distinguish between the two because he has no acceptance as a "naked" self—that is, he has no identity apart from his interaction with his environment.

He despairs in his dark moments because nothing seems to be "working out." But this is a personal reproach rather than a judgment concerning a project. As a perfectionist he naturally has great ambitions—in the parlance of the seminary, he had hoped to convert the world. Not only is he a proclaimer of the Messiah, but he has a touch of a Messiah complex. The limited success of most projects is the handwriting on the wall concerning the rather small role in life that is probably to be his. He is one among others rather than the one above others and it is hard to take. We may see this same identification with the project among the lay leaders. For such the "project thermometer" is really a "status thermometer." The feelings of the chairman may become of more concern to the pastor than the outcome of the project itself.

Troubles with the Lay People

The same difficulty of the pastor to accept himself apart from his accomplishments causes him problems also in relating to his people. They too fall below his expectations, and he may show the same impatience toward them that he shows toward himself. Actually their failures are in a sense his failures. Irked by their inadequate response, he may abandon inspiration as a means for motivating them and try instead to move them by guilt. Since guilt is the driving force behind the perfectionist, it is only logical that he would attempt to stimulate it in others when they appear to lag. Yet, obvious attempts to make people feel guilty normally backfire. They sense it as coercion and react defensively. What results is a widening breach between the minister who uses his authority as his right to criticize and the congregation that wards off his blows with passive defiance.

This unfortunate state of affairs is rarely the way the pastor-congregation relationship is initiated. Rather it is the way it may become. The relationship usually begins on a neutral basis or even a positive basis. The exception might occur when the congregation has not reconciled itself to the departure of the former pastor or when they feel the new pastor has been foisted upon them by dubious procedure. Normally, however, the initial air is one of hopeful expectancy on the part of both parties.

The Dangers of Overfamiliarity

This very expectancy, however, can lead to a premature intimacy. The minister who needs to be well liked tends to be a poor judge of people. He follows the overtures of those who are initially the most aggressive, as though he were merely a response to a stimulus. His attention is absorbed by the "waving flags." When ties are developed so quickly they may soon reach a stage of overfamiliarity. The intimacy is more than the relationship can endure because of the insufficient time to develop its roots. It may then turn sour. Those who were "thick as thieves" may cool off considerably.

There may be other built-in limitations to the pastor's intimacy with specific individuals. The pastor is an important person in the congregation. Those who are his intimates tend to "cash in" on his status. For some this constitutes the means for securing power. They become possessive toward him. Most relationships have their "use" value, but in these instances it is dominant. The pastor may also be guilty of needing such support: otherwise, would he allow the relationship to become so possessive? It is questionable whether intimacy based on use value can permit freedom of individuality. Should differences of view regarding church matters arise between the pastor and such a layman, tensions would soon develop. Their previous warmth would make their clash the more bitter. Both parties—and often their families—feel a sense of betrayal in the break. The experience is unpleasant, disillusioning, sour. Unfortunately their feelings may be projected toward the congregation as a whole.

There is also a built-in group limitation to these possessive relationships. The minister is the pastor of all the people. He cannot be an ally of the few or the center of a select—and often self-chosen—inner circle. As the other members of the congregation observe the development of these close relationships between the pastor and certain members, they may not view it with indifference. Since they are likely to have been in the congregation longer than the pastor, they may honestly question the wisdom of the pastor's alliances. He is their pastor too. Involuntarily they may resent these special intimacies, since by contrast their relationship is made to seem more distant. So they tend to withdraw still further, and leave the pastor even more dependent upon the intimate few.

What they should do is just the opposite. Actually most pastors really want to spread out in their fellowship, but may need the layman's help to do it. By continuing to show their concern for him and his welfare in spite of their emotional desire to withdraw, these members are actually assisting him in broadening his involvements, so that he does not become overly dependent upon the few.

"They Idolize, They Tantalize, They Scandalize."

The souring process may extend to the pastor's relationship to the congregation as a whole. One pastor described it in terms of a three-year process. "The first year they idolize me, the second year they tantalize me, and the third year they scandalize me." Since they do not know him very well the first year, they can think more highly of him than they ought to think. This is particularly true if they had trouble with the preceding minister. They then have a need to see the new minister in a contrastingly favorable light to justify themselves in their previous conflict.

But even beyond this, people have a need to think that there is someone who is better than they are—who is above the corruption that they are likely to know only too well. The minister is a likely candidate for such needed admiration. But because it is tantamount to deification, their attitude will undergo some adjustment as time reveals the minister's common humanity. The new broom always sweeps clean. Yet the slow deterioration of this highly idealized beginning is a sad and familiar story.

This deterioration in relationships is often referred to in matrimonial terms. "The honeymoon," we say, "is over." Unlike marriage, however, the relationship between pastor and congregation has no courtship period. From the beginning they are already "under contract." This means that the infatuation normally experienced in the first stage of courtship takes place "within the marriage." For many people, the new pastor appears to be a savior. Just to have him in the congregation promises to answer most of the problems of the congregation. To the pastor, the new congregation has a childlike appeal. The people seem like the ideal congregation, innocent, uncomplicated, and he looks forward to his ministry to them with high anticipation.

The second year is the year of tantalization. The honeymoon is still on but like the legendary character from whom we have derived the word *tantalize*, the fulfillment of expectations keeps eluding both parties. Because he had offended the gods, *Tantalus* had to stand up to his neck in water, which flowed from him when he tried to drink it. At the same time a bunch of fruit hung over his head, but the wind took it beyond his grasp every time he reached for it. The promise is still there—the hope is yet alive. But the fulfillment keeps eluding both pastor and people.

The third year they scandalize each other. When hopes go too high, the disillusion that follows is too low. Neither has received from the other what he had anticipated. The people whom the minister viewed as innocent now seem to have no innocence at all. Instead they are schemers out to thwart him. The man whom the people thought was a savior now cannot save and becomes instead an object of scorn. In this disillusioned stage the members refer to the pastor by his last name, shorn of any respectful or affectionate titles. Each has fallen from the unrealistic top rung of the ladder to the equally unrealistic bottom rung. Now that the honeymoon is over, the previous adulation may turn into malicious attack. It seems we have to get both extremes out of our system before we can adjust to reality.

In marriage much of this adjustment is worked out in the courtship. When it is postponed until after marriage, the adjustment is much more difficult because both parties feel trapped by the arrangement. They are stuck with it! But actually the period of scandalizing is a transition period out of which the relationship can mature to the point where each can take the other as he is. There is none who is innocent; nor can any be a savior. No one can play angel and no one can play God. The evil within us that poisons our relationships has to be faced and accepted. There is need for forgiveness on both sides. When our eyes are opened to reality and our expectations are in line with reality, relationships between people cannot only be maintained but can even grow in their meaningfulness.

Transference of Traumas

The pastor may also have problems in his relationships because he transfers traumatic relationships from his past to comparable people in his congregation. There are enough people in most congregations to produce great enough variety in personal types so that transference is unavoidable. An example of such is the pastor's image of the "big layman." This is the man who wants to "run the church" and "bulldozes" the minister in the process. The experience can be agonizing to the pastor. If he was bullied as a child by a parent or a sibling, and was never able to assert himself, he will usually find a bullying personality in every congregation. The minister's unrecognized hostility toward such a person is revealed by his anxiety to please him. Yet, the harder he tries, the more the hidden hostility slips out in "unintended" ways. The result is the usual strain in the relationship. What follows is the usual bullying, which seems unjustified to the minister because of his efforts to please, with the victim once again nursing his wounds and feeling sorry for himself. It seems that his enemy has triumphed over him and God is letting it happen.

There is always the hope that these traumas will not continually repeat themselves in meaningless cycles, but that, as is possible in all crises, the truth may break through. Life is not simply a drama of cruel giants and innocent victims, for the victim himself helps to create the giant. Our own resentful imagination has much to do with our image of being persecuted. As Martin Niemöller, himself a victim of persecution, put it, "It has taken me a long time to learn that God is not the enemy of my enemies. He is not even the enemy of *his* enemies." When one is delivered from the fear of the black giant, he realizes that the giant was not nearly so large or so black as he had seemed.

But this does not mean that this bullying layman exists simply as a projection of the pastor's mind. There are laymen who would like to use the congregation as a resource for power. The minister may stand in the way of this power. The question before such a layman is whether he shall accept the leadership position of the pastor or neutralize this leadership by aligning himself with it, or whether he should oppose it by attacking the pastor. Most people will make their peace when they have met their match. But perhaps here also the light may break through. Why does one need to wield power? What inner lack is he compensating for by this need to run things? And where does Christ's teaching about the one who would be greatest being as a child— rather than childish—enter the picture?

The Difficulties with Men

The ministry is a man's profession. Men have seen to that! From St. Paul to the present governing boards of many of our denominations—usually predominately male—the ordination of women to the ministry is frowned upon. Those denominations that ordain women do so very infrequently, and the majority of ordained women are not serving as pastors of congregations. Many are married to ordained men and serve in a marital partnership.

There is some justification for this discrimination. Religion seems to be a feminine subject. The prescribed male leadership may seem ironic on this basis, but it is also a protection. If there were no such prescription, the remaining masculine identification with religion could disappear. Religiously speaking, the principle seems to be that where there are men, there will also be women, but where there are women, there may not also be men. In most families the mother is the dominant religious influence. Mother Monica praying for her son Augustine's conversion is a familiar family symbol. Father is more interested in his son's becoming a successful businessman or lawyer. The old revival song, "Tell Mother I'll be There [Heaven]," would draw little response if it were "Tell Father I'll be There." While God is called Father in the Christian religion, the persistent attempts to bring in the mother image as the Church or as the Virgin Mary show this same religious pull toward the feminine.

The mother image is important for Protestants as well as Catholics. Unfortunately for both, the idea of God as Father makes it necessary to find the mother image elsewhere. Catholics find it in the exaltation of the Virgin Mary and Protestants add it to their image of Jesus. God may discipline, but Jesus is comforting. Mother Mary will pray for us.

Though the ministry is a man's profession, the minister may find it hard to relate to men. Since religion has a particularly feminine appeal, he already has one strike against him. His own religious interests may have come more from his mother than his father. Although his relationship with women is more complicated, he may find he feels more at ease with women than men. The exception would be the "masculine" woman. If religion attracts the feminine more than the masculine, the man who chooses a religious profession is himself of a different caste. For one thing he is made to feel different. Even as a school boy he notices raised eyebrows when he mentions that he plans to be a minister. People can accept it better if he comes from the parsonage, because then he is already different. Perhaps, also, he is made to feel set apart because he *is* set apart. Religion concerns the *holy* and holy means set apart. We approach it with awe. When Pope Paul VI visited India, the Hindus were eager to see him because he is by his profession a "holy man."

The Feminine Qualities

But is the difference only in the attitude of people toward a "holy" profession? Even the personality sciences put his interests in a special category. On the Minnesota Multiphasic Personality Inventory, which many colleges and seminaries administer to the theological student, he tends to have a "high mf"—that is, to be characterized by feminine as well as masculine qualities. Every man has feminine as well as masculine qualities, even as every woman has masculine as well as feminine qualities. Without this balance within them they would find it difficult to establish any relationship with those of the opposite sex. The theological student, however, tends to have these feminine qualities in a more pronounced way.

But what are these "feminine" qualities in the Minnesota

Multiphasic Personality Inventory? They are interests in religion and the arts—in people more than things—in feelings as well as logic. In contrast the masculine characteristics center in interests in science, mathematics, blueprints, the sports page, and mystery stories. Religion is closely associated with music and the arts. Poetry and music come together in hymn singing. Drama and music join in liturgy. Religious themes provide the finest expression in painting and sculpture. The religious person is often a meditative person, and by this fact, appreciative of the inner life, of reflection. He is an imaginative person whose sermons are works of art that fill the hearer with inspiration.

Does the more lonely person tend to choose the ministry? Does the more sensitive man tend to choose it? Is the minister more inclined to be an artist than a scientist? There are men in the ministry who could fit any category. There are former mechanics, scientists, football players, engineers, boxers, and construction workers. But these do not constitute the familiar pastoral image. Therefore, when the football star decides on the ministry, this makes him unique—even newsworthy. In spite of his masculine identification, the aura of the holy tends to separate him from the world of men in the popular mind. Because he needed the money, a pastor in a large urban center took a construction job during his vacation. For the first week he remained incognito. Listening to the unaffected conversation of his fellow workmen, he discovered it centered on sex, drink, and sports. During the second week his identity was discovered. From then on the conversation centered on sports.

Unearned Leadership

The minister is given a position of leadership without earning it from the people he leads. Upon his graduation from seminary he is called to lead a group of people whom he probably has never met. He may not be a natural leader—

few people are. He may have conflicts over his superimposed authority, particularly around men. In contrast, the lay leaders of the congregation have come up through the ranks. They usually have demonstrated some natural leadership ability. Feeling the pressure from his leadership shortcomings, the pastor is tempted to take shortcuts to bolster his position. He may become authoritarian in his approach to compensate for his insecurity in the leadership role. Called to leadership in the congregation on the basis of his office, the minister fulfills his leadership on the basis of his person. If he feels inadequate to lead, he may find it easier to strengthen his office than to strengthen his personal relationships. Those who find persuasion difficult tend to resort to coercion.

The Latest Challenge

The minister is discovering an increasing challenge in relating to people in the growing number of parishes with more than one minister. Because of the strain in working with another person, these partnerships have at times created serious disturbances. With our growing population and denominational mergers we can expect the number of team ministry parishes to increase. Other professions have had a longer history in working together than has the Protestant ministry. Barbers, teachers, physicians, and lawyers have all had to learn to work together in the same shop, school, clinic, and office. But here also I imagine that occasional tensions mar the harmony. The customer's preference for one barber over another in the same shop has been known to irritate the barber who must stand by his empty chair while the customer waits for his partner to finish. Medical clinics have been known to have their staff personality clashes. Teachers can become jealous of the popularity of other teachers. Without a history in working together, the ministerial profession has found it more difficult than these other professionals, despite their common humanity.

The structure of the congregational life tends to encourage whatever prima donna characteristics a pastor may possess. His preaching is a form of performance for which he may be complimented. He may even be referred to as "the preacher." We speak of some ministers as "pulpiteers." There are churches that are referred to by the minister's name. It is Stark's church, or the church where Dr. Stark is the preacher. The personal magnetism of the minister is a strong element in his success. In contrast to the less effective minister who hides his person behind his office, the more successful minister may overshadow the office with his person. People may return after departing the community to have him baptize their children. He may be called from afar to perform marriages. The bereaved desire *him* to conduct the funeral. The touch of his person seems to provide an added charisma to the ministerial act.

These are the extremes that the pastor's personal appeal can take as he becomes a part of the life of a community. Obviously there is not much room for two such "personality giants" in one congregation. Therefore not everybody can work in a team ministry situation. Perhaps we need more time for developing certain personality inventories specifically designed to determine whether certain ministers can work together. In spite of the mechanical factor in such prognoses, they are to be desired in preference to the conflicts that can divide a church in its loyalties.

The frequent combination is the older and successful minister who has a younger or even beginning minister as his assistant. The older man has learned much the hard way. He has developed a certain *modus operandi* that he believes is effective. In contrast, the younger man is in the process of establishing himself and desires to strike out on his own. He has ideas—new ideas—and he wants to try them out. The older man may feel he has already explored them and found them wanting. "We tried that some ten years ago," he says, "and it just didn't work." But the young man wants the freedom to make his own mistakes. On the other hand the older man does not want his own mistakes repeated. How shall they work out this difficult tension which seems to be built into the arrangement rather than the fault of either one?

Again, the Laymen Hold the Key

The layman may hold the key to the answer. Both pastors are particularly sensitive to the feelings of the people. Both may also have to suffer a few adjustment pains. The way to resolve these tensions is for the parties involved to talk out their feelings together. In a dark moment, however, one may make a careless complaint to the laymen. All that is needed now to create a major crisis is a few people with an unconscious bent for stirring up trouble. I do not believe any layman deliberately tries to provoke one pastor against another. Yet some may be doing it regardless. They lend a sympathetic ear to the momentary complaint and support the complainer's negative feelings toward the other person. The implication is—we are on your side. Where there are *sides* the conflict can only widen. When the conflict becomes known there are usually enough malcontents—neurotics if you will—in any congregation for a potential schism. They project their own internal conflicts onto the church conflict and play one pastor against the other. The question is, which pastor has the support of the people?

This can be a frightening experience for the older minister. He feels under attack where before he felt secure. Once the conflict is in the open, some will side with the younger man simply because he symbolizes the underdog. For the younger minister it is a frustrating experience. To him it seems his adversary is well entrenched and therefore rebellion is futile. Unfortunately most of us like the excitement of strife and unwittingly encourage it by making it the major subject in congregational conversation.

If, however, the lay leaders would direct their energies toward assuring both men of their support as a team, encourage each man in private to make allowances for the stage in life of the other, and express their feelings honestly to each other in love, they would be facilitating the adjustment that might lead to harmony. They can also discourage the gossiplike conversation that corrupts the participators as much as any open strife.

Whatever crisis the ministry is now experiencing, it is aggravated by the minister's own personality problems as these pertain to his self-acceptance and his ability to relate to his neighbor as a person and as a man.

V. NEED FOR A SUCCESSFUL FAMILY

Like any other marriage, the minister's marriage has its ups and downs, its periods of tension and of harmony. This puts a strain upon the wife, not because her husband is a pastor, but because he is *her* pastor. Psychiatrist Margaretta Bowers, whose services are utilized by many ministers and their wives, says that it would be a relief for the wife if she could attend some other church than her husband's during times of marital stress, so that the minister could serve as a "good symbol" for her. But, as she admits, tradition insists the wife should attend her husband's services at *all* times.[1] So, from the husband with whom she is angry she must hear the Word and receive the Sacrament. The stress is also additionally hard on the husband because he is a minister. He loses respect for himself as a minister when he knows his wife does not respect him. He feels defeated and insincere. While it is difficult for her to listen to him preach during these times, it is equally difficult for him to preach, knowing she is listening. These internal pressures upon the minister's family life, which are aggravated by his office, are further aggravated by the external pressures which stem directly from his office.

In line with the pressure to succeed in his career, the minister is under pressure to have a successful family life. In fact he *has* to have it. "For if a man know not how to rule his own home, how shall he take care of the church of God?" (I Tim. 3:5) How can he expect to guide others in their marriage and family if his own marriage and family are not exemplary? As the pastor of a congregation his family life is much more on display than if he were a marriage and family counselor. Under this pressure he may become increasingly critical toward his family for any deviation of behavior and attempt to coerce them to conform. His wife may also feel this pressure and exploit the children in the same manner. "What will people think!" The children who hear this may not feel kindly disposed toward these "people" or toward the lot into which an inconsiderate providence has placed them. It may seem that they are simply an extension of their father's pastoral prestige and pastoral ego.

The parsonage family feels the pressure to be an example in their conduct because they belong to the man whose profession it is to be an example. The concept of the minister as an example leads to an unhealthy differentiation between the pastor and the people. It is this differentiation that is passed on to his family—and they resent it. The minister's differentiation is not his example but his being called by the congregation to serve as their leader in the congregation's ministry. The faith that they hold in common is comparable to the life that they have in common. The "difference" is not between pastor and people but between believer and non-believer. When this difference centers on the pastor, his family may feel they are being "used" rather than loved. His need for their cooperation gives them a club if they desire to hit back. Then what will people think!

The pastor's family is an easy target for criticism. When a certain minister resigned from his parish for no apparent reason, the community was curious. Why had he done so? The conclusion was that it must have been because of his wife. Why? What else could it have been? Lacking the authoritative role of her husband, the minister's wife may even receive criticism meant for him. An outspoken wife of an Anglican clergyman calls this situation the church's double standard. "I resent the basic reason behind it," she said, "that somehow we are different."[2]

The children are also singled out. When involved in offenses, they are likely to receive the spotlight. Even parsonage families that play down this differentiation at home feel the pressure on their children from the outside. I know of one parsonage wife in particular who was determined that her children were going to be reared without this differentiation. Imagine her feelings when her boy was called on the carpet along with others at school for a misdemeanor, and the principal said to him before them all, "You of all people should be ashamed of yourself, for you are a minister's son!"

Because he is emotionally identified both with his family and with his vocation, the minister may become hostile toward his family and his congregation when these criticisms are voiced. He is irked at the congregation for criticizing those who belong to him, and feels alienated from them because of it. At the same time he is irritated with his family for leaving themselves open to criticism. The situation is embarrassing because it "rocks the boat." It is not difficult for an administratively minded minister to conceive of his function in terms of promoting harmony. When the family then exposes him to criticism, they add to his burden. He fears the specter of his own tarnished public image. Should this be the shadow he most fears, his family may feel he would sell them out before risking his pastoral prestige.

The Neglected Wife

The conflict of loyalties between family obligations and congregational obligations is difficult to avoid under normal circumstances, but when the pastor exploits his family to satisfy his own need for success, it is even worse. Although his family receives attention because of him, this can hardly compensate for their *own* sense of worth. In fact this appendage type of attention can hinder this sense of worth. Pauline Trueblood voiced the lament of the professional man's wife when she said, "It has been my privilege to converse with many wives in my travels with my husband. I am always on the fringes of every public occasion which

we attend, meeting the other women who are also on the
fringes. We all know what it is to have our husbands introduced, with the opportunity of making a reply, while we
are introduced in a manner which assumes that we are unable to make any response at all. We rise and smile. Personally I should rather be ignored. If I could say even a few
words I should feel more like a human being."[3] Mrs. Trueblood is complaining about the "feminine mystique" which
Betty Friedan attacks—that the wife lives through her husband and children rather than establishing an identity of
her own.[4] Being partakers in the minister's opportunities
may hinder the minister's family from having their own
opportunities as individuals with their own identity.

If he gives little thought to the needs of his family beyond
his professional concerns, the minister may soon have the
burden of the unhappy wife who resents not so much his
vocation as his attitude toward his vocation. Because of it
she feels neglected—even "sinned" against. She has a rival
for his affections and is jealous—ironically, of the Lord. Her
husband is worse than a bigamist because his work comes
first. She may have begun her marriage while her husband
was in seminary or even in college, and may have worked
to help him get through seminary. She may have been understanding when he neglected her for his studies, for she could
look forward to the day when school would be over and they
could settle down to a normal life.

But it never happened. Instead the busy student became
the busy minister, and had even better reasons for his neglect. Accustomed by then to the grind, he kept up the same
work pace and found one emergency after another to justify
it. Having now no future to look forward to as she had in
seminary days, she feels trapped and disillusioned. In reaction she may begin to whine and nag at him for more time
and attention. But whining and nagging only drive him
further into his work.

Despite her obvious deprivation she finds it hard to justify her resentment. It is bad enough that his work is important. What frustrates her is that it is religious. She and the children may feel guilty that they begrudge the church his time and energy. They may be unable to express their complaint directly until they are emotionally distraught. Yet their resentment eats away inside them, hindering their own interest and involvement in the church.

The wife of the Anglican clergyman to which we previously referred is an exception to this usual containment. When she married, she said, she had high-minded visions of entering with her husband into the great work of converting the world. "But here I am [seven years later]," she said, "surrounded by four children, tied to the house, expected to turn up at every cat hanging and feeling like a widow as my husband is always on duty." Her conclusion is unequivocal. "Clergymen," she said, "ought to be celibate because no decent right-minded man ought to have the effrontery to ask any woman to take on a lousy job. It is thoroughly un-Christian."[5]

And Neglected Children

The harassed clergyman may find himself torn between his ordination vow and his marriage vow. The fact that families tend to be larger today adds to the problem. Since World War II the number of children per family has been increasing, particularly in the urban, professional, and managerial social groups.[6] With the marriage beginning in seminary or even in college, the contemporary minister is likely to have children by the time he enters the ministry. The vast building programs of the Church since World War II also add to the problem. He is needed more at home because of the children and needed more at church because of the increase in administrative responsibilities.

The pastor shares the common problem of fathers whose work leaves them little time or energy for creative family living. The man is by nature vocationally oriented. His family role is secondary. But this differentiation is compounded for the minister as well as others whose work is a never-ending drain upon their time and energy. Since the problem goes beyond the parsonage family, it is one which the congregation could work on together. The family of the commuting father can understand the parsonage family. By the time he spends a couple of nights a week at the church and works late at the office a couple more, he has little time or energy left for the family. The Church is more than an institution and its activities go further than the church building. The Church is also family life and church work should not compete with it. Otherwise we may find ourselves in the unfortunate position of pitting the institution of the Church against the institution of the family rather than placing the Church in the family.

The Congregation Can Help

The congregation can help the pastor to cultivate his family life. The minister's schedule is different from most others. The weekend is his heavy time. Because the majority of people work during the day, much of his ministry is in the evening. This leaves him opportunities for his family that are not available to most men. If his wife can manage it, and providing the children are home for lunch, he may eat most of his meals with his family. But this in itself may not mean much unless he is present in more than body. The challenge is to make eating together a time for fellowship together. If he takes Monday as his day off to be with his wife and pre-school children, he does not have to contend with the weekend crowds in the recreational areas. Yet he hopes that people who see him realize that this is his day off and that he is not neglecting his work simply because he has no time clock to punch.

Most professional and businessmen have work to do in

the evenings. Therefore the supper hour and the early evening should be reserved for the family. The time for meetings could be arranged to permit this. Also, unless it is necessary, this time should not be interrupted by phone calls. If mealtime is to be a relaxing time, it cannot be in competition with the telephone. The children who were counting on this time with Dad resent the ringing noise that takes him away. As the book of Ecclesiastes says, there is a time for everything—including using the phone.

The congregation might also consider having fewer meetings. The time wasted in meetings is tragic. If people prepared for meetings, they would not take so long and there would be fewer of them. Some meetings, of course, are essential. But the minister should not be expected to attend each and every one of them. The evening hours are the best time for pastoral counseling and calling. It is poor stewardship of his time to use this strategic time for a meeting that laymen with any degree of competence should be able to handle. When the pastor feels he has more important things to do than attend a particular meeting, he should not be made to feel that he is neglecting his duty. He must have the freedom to decide which of his conflicting obligations is the more pastoral.

The Value of Guilt Feelings

Besides the guilt he feels over neglecting his wife, the minister may also feel guilty over neglecting his children. He hopes that being in the Lord's work means that the Lord will make up for his neglect. He feels uneasy even though he tries to justify himself. "What else can I do?" he asks. The purpose of guilt is to draw our attention to the contrast between the way things are and the way they should be, so that we might take action to close the gap. If the minister is not able to take this action, he can justifiably question his guilt.

But is he really so unable? Guilt that leads to no action may indicate that one is afraid to act—or is at least not ready to act. Should he act, he might change and this would make his past all the more indefensible. Our inaction is often a subconscious defense of our past omissions. On the other hand, should he act, his guilt might be resolved. His inaction may mean that he is not ready to be without his guilt. Though it makes us uncomfortable, guilt provides a continuity with the past. When one feels guilty, he knows where he stands, even though he stands under judgment. He feels guilty over *something*. He has something to confess—something of which to repent. Guilt implies that our life has meaning, though we have not lived up to it. In this judgment we have an identity.

For many of us, our guilt is bound up with our sense of meaning. It is the assurance that we are accountable to something or someone that is bigger than we are. If our guilt should be removed, the life to which we are accustomed would be changed. This can be frightening—for what, if anything, would it change into? The greatest dread is not the dread of *something*, but the dread of *nothing*. The greatest fear is of the unknown. We may have our misgivings over our ruts, but we are at home with them. We have been this way before.

The demands of the ministry provide an easy out for those who resist being with their families. The press of duties gives to their conscience its desired sop. Some men shy away from giving themselves to their wife and children. This problem is not simply a minister's problem—but a man's problem. He is afraid of intimacy and keeps busy to avoid it. These men have a hard time on weekends or holidays when they are not working. They pace—become irritated if not agitated—get headaches. Moonlighting is one way to avoid the situation. The need for more money, of course, is given as the reason, but again, few of us can stand to admit that we are running from intimacy with ourselves and our loved ones. The pastor does not have to moonlight. His vocation takes care of that. There are always enough pressing situations in any parish to give a "good out" to the man who wants it. If he has a resistance to family intimacy, he can with good reason say, "What else can I do?"

A Problem for Everybody

Since the number of jobs is continuing to decrease because of automation, the problem of leisure time is going to increase. Men are faced not only with the problem of making a living, but with learning to live. Pastor and congregation together can work on this problem, for besides being a common problem, it is a religious problem.

People have problems in family living which they would not have if they were frequently absent from the home. This has been my own experience when travel engagements have interfered with my home responsibilities. When the man is frequently absent, the family learns to function without him. He becomes an outsider who can come and go and the family living goes on much the same. If, however, he stays around long enough to be taken seriously by the family, he is going to become involved in the family tensions. The greater intimacy puts a strain on his relationships—even the children have to come to terms with his presence—but it is the only way to deepen these relationships. As one minister's son said, "I had a pastor, but not a father."

The man in charge in the congregation may be "out of it" at home. Whether or not his wife is a partner to his ineffectiveness, her own function in the family becomes distorted because of it. When she functions for both parents, particularly when the father is around, she becomes less feminine. Obviously this decline in femininity is no encouragement to the *marital* relationship.

The problem of the ineffective father is not confined to parsonage families. Modern man has a difficult time identifying himself with any definite role in the family circle. He is inclined to move or be pushed to the periphery, leaving the center to mother. The organizations of the congregation could discuss this common family problem with profit. The parsonage family could join with others in sharing ways and means for strengthening the masculine influence in family living.

The minister's need for a successful family may actually interfere with the kind of effort that is needed to have such a family. If he involves himself in the life of his family he is likely to see the family problems—and this is threatening to his image of a successful family. Instead he may choose to live under the illusion that problems that are not recognized will go away. Because of his profession he is reluctant to seek help when help is obviously needed. Should he admit to these problems, he may feel he is exposing himself as a professional failure.

The Wife's Specific Problems

One of the advantages that the minister's wife has over other professional wives is that she is involved with her husband in his work. She feels responsible, even as he does, for the life of the congregation. Their vocational sharing should enhance the in-commonness of their marriage. However, it also presents obstacles to in-commonness. If a man gets "steamed up" at his boss or fellow workers at the plant, he can "let it off" to his wife because she is not personally involved at the plant. The pastor, however, may be reluctant to express his frustrations with the people of his congregation to his family. His wife and children have their own relationships with these people and he does not want to color them by his own momentary frustrations. How can he expect his wife, for example, to continue to be cordial to people who are "abusing" her husband?

There is also the possibility that the vocational partnership may become synonymous with the marital partnership. There is the danger in every marriage that the business of rearing a family and establishing a home may crowd out the couple's companionship as husband and wife. The parsonage marriage has, in addition, this vocational partnership, and there may not seem to be either the time or the opportunity for cultivating the marriage as such.

The minister's wife is often confused about her role as minister's wife. She may wonder what is expected of her. Unfortunately she has little to go on to find out. The Reformation created the parsonage but left its structure undefined, and there is still little in the way of a blueprint. Opinions on her function vary from complete involvement in parish life to little but a passive involvement. She is left largely on her own to struggle over which responsibilities come first. One wife queried in a research study said she had come to the conclusion that her first responsibility was to her children. "They are entitled," she said with tongue in cheek, "to at least one parent who is willing and able to put their development and interests first."[7] The obvious implication is—why not two parents?

The congregation can help the pastor's wife in her struggle for her own identity by letting her be an individual. It is poor psychology to play up the pastor's predecessor to the pastor and it is downright unfair to compare the pastor's wife to her predecessor. It is the minister who has been called by the congregation—not his wife. She should be given the freedom to do what comes naturally to her personality in establishing her role in the congregation.

The tension that builds up from these pressures upon the parsonage family can keep the atmosphere of the home from being a haven for emotional release and satisfaction. When the wife feels neglected as a wife, she begins to resent the time he spends with others. "Why," she asks, "is he so concerned about Mrs. Smith's marital problems and not mine?" Surveys indicate that what the minister's wife dislikes most about her lot in life is the lack of family time. The tension thwarts the satisfaction of the family's need for affection—and also the minister's need for affection. There is a connection between a man's morale in his home and his morale in his work. If his home atmosphere is understanding in this regard, he is able to return to his work in a better frame of mind. But if the home adds to his frustration, he may descend to the abyss of despair. "What's the use?" he says—the pastoral equivalent of "What the hell!"

Sexual Transgressions

In this frame of mind he is open to the temptations that present themselves to any man whose work involves him in close contact with the opposite sex. It is home conditions such as these that lead to the mental temptations or even indiscreet actions that plague some men in their ministry. Sexual deviations are more likely to occur with a sexually unsatisfied minister than with one whose married life is characterized by affection and understanding. The minister may not realize his emotional deprivation until he is tempted. The press of duties may keep his discontent out of his focus until he begins to find satisfaction in someone else. The reason some of us may drive ourselves in our work is to divert our attention from our own emptiness. Seduction usually begins in companionship, and the sexual aspect is the follow-up. The results can be tragic. Because sex is an expression of affection, sexual temptations are particularly perturbing to those who are lacking in this affection. The minister who neglects his marriage for his work is endangering his work as well as his marriage.

Anyone whose work places him in intimate associations with those of the opposite sex needs to be a committed person. While his commitment does not prevent his being tempted, it does provide the inner strength to control his actions. The pastor as a human being is subject to all human temptations; he also has the same needs as others. It is his duty to his commitment to see that these needs are met in the most wholesome ways available to him, so that he will not be susceptible to opportunities that are destructive.

The minister needs the affection of his family as much as they need his. Most of the problems of the unhappy wife are cured by more love, time, and affection from her husband. But before he can give or receive this affection, his family members have to become ends in themselves and not means to an end. It is only as the minister gives up the egocentric need to have a successful family for the sake of his professional reputation that he can begin to love and enjoy his family as values in themselves. His love for his wife as a woman rather than as his right arm in his vocation helps to give her the identity that she needs. His love for his children as individuals committed to him by God gives to them the freedom they need to discover their own religious identity.

VI. THE NEED TO BE A LEADER IN THE FAITH

We have mentioned the similarity between the problems of the businessman and those of the minister. This does not mean, however, that his problems are *nothing but* the problems of the businessman. The demands upon the minister are similar to those upon other professional men, but at least in one respect they are unique. The minister is a leader in faith. The qualities for this demand are deeply personal. Faith is a matter of one's spirit—one's commitment.

The Unique Challenge

His leadership in faith is different than having administrative ability, speaking ability, or even personality appeal. The good administrators, orators, and salesmen in the ministry could succeed equally well in other social and business enterprises. His abilities help to make him a *capable* pastor, but they do not make him a pastor. We note a similar situation with the lay leader. The qualities that make for leadership in the church also make for leadership in the community—in service clubs, chambers of commerce, women's clubs, P.T.A.'s, and the like, and it is not unusual to find the same people occupying both civic and church leadership positions. But again, the church leader has the unique responsibility of being a leader in *faith,* and despite its external manifestations, faith belongs to the inner man.

The clergyman's leadership in faith also has its external manifestations. At the same time this leadership cannot be identified with such accomplishments as building a parish house, increasing the membership roll, and successful promotion of the program. The difference is between what a person can do—achieve—and what he is—in his being. This demand directs him to his own naked self for his justification. Most of us feel more at ease if we can have a few accomplishments to bolster our justification as a person. But to stand transparent before God with nothing in hand—no adornments and even no recommendations—leaves one with nothing but the grace of God. A veteran minister related an experience from his early ministry that had left its mark in his memory. He was asked by a comparative stranger if he were a Christian. "I'm a Lutheran minister," he replied. The stranger was not satisfied. "That's not what I asked you," he said.

This minister was shaken by the experience because it forced him to go from the outer man where he felt secure to the inner man where he felt less sure of himself. When he looks within himself, the minister may not always see faith, but rather the doubts he would try to silence in anyone else. He sees also the egocentric motivations which he condemns from the pulpit, and the agonizing question keeps recurring, "Whose glory am I really seeking?" When one's religion is also his profession, it is hard for him to know how much of his religion is his *apart* from his profession and how much is his *because* of his profession.

The defender of *faith* would also like to have more support from *sight*. While, according to the Scripture, we walk not by sight but by faith, we seem to feel more sure of our faith when we have some tangible evidence for it. As a professional religionist, the minister is continually burning his bridges behind him—putting himself out on a limb—in the pulpit, in the Bible class, at the sickbed, and at the graveside. Always his is the "sure and certain hope." He assumes the responsibility of an aggressive commitment—the responsibility of a leader—a leader in faith. Questions that are threatening to this faith are also threatening to his leadership. Defensively he may push them aside and content

himself with the apparent sureness of his own religious authorities. He may feel strengthened in faith by joining with
these authorities in attacking opposing positions. Likewise
he may experience a real boost to his faith when he receives
support from other and unexpected sources.

The atmosphere today however, is not congenial to the
prejudiced mind. Questions which the minister may arbi-
trarily dismiss because they contradict his beliefs do not stay
dismissed; rather they increase in intensity to the point that
they may break down his defense system. Since he is not
prepared for such an assault, his faith may sag. In despair
he may turn against the authorities upon which he formerly
depended.

The problem goes back again to the minister's image of
himself—and the pressure to live up to this image. Others
are looking to him to affirm the faith. They want him to be
sure so that they can be sure. But expected behavior is con-
trolled behavior. It is based on the assumption that the outer
implies the inner. Yet, the outer may also contradict the
inner. One's assertion of certainty may be his attempt to
quiet his inner doubt. In this dependence upon the leader's
sureness, the real nature of faith as a leap is lost. The way to
sureness in faith is not through dispelling uncertainty, but
through facing uncertainty. Our faith is maintained not by
our defenses, but by our honesty in confronting our doubts.

The Pastor Is Human, but . . .

It is difficult to identify with anyone whom we regard as
an authority. God became a man in order to identify with
mankind. But mankind has found it hard to accept this
identification. The difficulty in accepting the divinity of
Christ has not been as great for his followers as the difficulty in accepting his humanity. Even a sinless humanity is
difficult to accept, because being sinless does not mean being free from temptation. Was Jesus tempted in all points as

we are? By sex? By unbelief? Similarly, it is hard for the lay-man to accept the sinfulness of his pastor. The saints seem superhuman. Intellectually he can accept the fact that his pastor is a sinner. "He's a human being just like us," he says. But to accept this emotionally is another matter.

Most of us would like to think that there is someone around who is better than we are. The likely candidate for this position is the minister. As one church councilman put it, "I know my pastor takes a drink—in fact I like him to have a drink with me. I know he's married—and therefore that he does—well, that he does certain things. This is all fine and dandy. But dawgone it!—I still want him to be up *there!*" As he said this he gestured with his hand slightly above his own head. "I want my minister to be a cut above *me.*"

The contradiction in this man's image of the pastor il-lustrates the confusion of the layman in this regard. On the one hand he wants his pastor to be a "good Joe"—to be as-sured of his humanity. At the same time he wants him to be a "cut above"—an assurance of his "superhumanity." This ambivalent expectation will frustrate any pastor who feels the pressure to fulfill it. A man whom a certain pastor wanted to interest in the church asked him to have a beer with him. The pastor had no strong feelings either way about beer, but he nevertheless declined. Subsequently he wondered whether or not he had missed an opportunity to identify with this man. On another occasion when the man asked him again he accepted. But as luck would have it, the man later informed him that he was disappointed in him for taking the beer because he felt that he really had not wanted it.

The same ambiguity pertains to the minister's anger. Most of us have a hard time dealing with anger and expect that the minister of all people should control his temper—if it should be conceivable that he has one. In discussing this point a group of laymen were voicing the general feeling that, while they knew that the minister became angry like everybody else, it bothered them when he showed his anger. One of their number, however, admitted that there were times when he liked to see his pastor angry. "Our minister preaches his best sermons," he said, "when he's mad!" Some of us need to be scolded to alleviate the agitation of our guilt. At the same time some ministers may become dynamic only when empowered by anger. While the wrath of man may not work the righteousness of God, it may temporarily integrate the preacher's energies.

Who Reassures the Minister?

The layman naturally looks up to the minister. He needs him as a source of strength and inspiration. The successful minister takes advantage of this. He knows that people want to be reassured about the validity of their faith—that God really is, that there really is a life beyond the grave, that all things really do work together for good to the believer. In his sermons and in his pastoral care he reassures them of these things. But who reassures the minister? And what really does his reassurance contribute?

Students coming to the seminary often expect to find the ideal community. Secretly they are hoping that the seminary environment will strengthen their faith. But after they become a part of this community they begin to realize that seminary students are like others, and they are disillusioned. Instead of finding people who were better than they were, they found those who were in their own situation, and even some who seemed to be worse off than they. Laymen might become disillusioned with ministers if they knew them intimately, because they want them to be different. They like the double standard—in fact they need it. If some are under the higher morality, the rest of us can be justified on a lower basis. There is less demand upon a *follower*.

In spite of our desire for a superhuman saintly class, the

same selfish, sensual, hostile, skeptical thoughts that go through the ordinary Christian's mind also go through the mind of the saint. The flesh of the minister is no different from the flesh of the layman. His fleshly desires are equally contrary to the desires of the Spirit, so that he, like the layman, cannot do the things that he would. Nevertheless, since he lives in the Spirit and not in the flesh, he is obligated as the layman to walk in the Spirit.

The fact that the minister is not on a higher plane bothers the minister as much as the layman. When he realizes that the same selfish, sensual, hostile thoughts go through his mind as go through the minds of those to whom he ministers, he also is disillusioned. "If I am a leader in faith," he says, "Heaven help us! But I *am!* What if the layman knew? It's bad enough that I know!" There are those times as he steps to his pulpit when the incongruity of it all is overwhelming. "What am I doing here? Who am I to be telling these people these things? What am I saying—and why?"

There is an advantage in the sinfulness of the pastor that both layman and pastor lose sight of in their disillusion. If somebody is a cut above me, he may not understand me. The fact that the pastor is in the flesh as well as in the Spirit means that he ought have no problem empathizing with any sinner. Such an empathic identification can be a real advantage in pastoral communication. It is much easier for the preacher to hold up the mirror if he has seen himself in it. When his message has relevancy for himself, it will also be relevant to others. They sense that he understands and are encouraged to confide in him.

Because of his own shortcomings the layman tends to demand too much of the pastor. Some of this demand may also be in reciprocation for being preached to—or at. We have an unconscious desire to pull down the authority—particularly the moral authority. While driving through a small town late at night I was stopped by a policeman for exceeding the speed limit. He treated me as a routine offender until he saw on my driver's license that I was a clergy-man. Although it was two o'clock in the morning and my family was with me, I was subjected to a twenty-minute lecture on the incongruity of a minister who would violate the law. He interspersed the lecture periodically with the threat that perhaps it would be more fitting if I were charged with reckless driving than simply with speeding. The fine then would be fifty dollars rather than ten. Although I will admit that it was difficult for me to be unbiased in this situ-ation, I sensed that the officer was getting a secret satisfac-tion out of turning the tables. How the mighty have fallen! People who have accrued for themselves the image of moral goodness are subjected to double censure when they fall from that image. The contrast provides the justification for which we apparently wait to attack those who seem to set themselves above us. The intensity of the attack indicates the need that it fulfills.

The difference in standards that are demanded by those who accept no such demands for themselves goes largely unchallenged. In the Swedish novel *Holy Masquerade* by Olov Hartmann, the wife of a minister makes no claim to be a Christian despite her position. Instead she devotes her energies to attacking her husband for his inconsistencies as a Christian leader. There was no doubt that the clergyman left himself vulnerable to her attacks. Yet it was easy for her, who would assume no responsibility, to attack him, who had committed himself to much responsibility. Although even the law excuses a wife from testifying against her husband, the clergyman's wife used her privilege of intimate knowl-edge as a club to destroy him.

Those who would never leave the safety of the trunk are the most eager to saw off the limb from under those who have ventured forth. As long as the minister is conceived as a leader in morality rather than as a herald of good news, he will be vulnerable to this secret desire of the many to pull down the exalted few. The layman who assumes leadership in his church faces the same situation at a less intense level. The religious responsibility to which his leadership commits him places him in a tenuous relationship with his fellows. They view him with that peculiar mixture of respect and derision that is the common lot of moral authorities. He receives the projection of their own conflicts over morality and authority figures.

The Desire to Please and the Desire to Destroy

While there is a desire to attack the religious authority, there is also the desire to please him. This ambivalence comes out in our attitude toward the minister's visit. On one occasion I called on a family whose name was given to me by a neighbor. I sensed the tension as I seated myself on the sofa and attempted to engage the family in conversation. Bringing my feet close to the sofa in a nervous movement, I kicked over a hastily concealed glass of whiskey and its contents flowed out onto the rug. Obviously I had called at an inopportune moment and they did not want me to get the wrong—or right—impression. I tried to dispel the tension with a few innocuous remarks, but there was no relieving the embarrassment as each person went in a different direction to get something with which to clean up the rug.

The humorous aspect of the minister's visit has not been missed by cartoonists. In the comic strip "Snuffy Smith," for example, Snuffy and his wife Loweezy were quarreling violently in the first few pictures. Then little Jughaid burst into the house to warn them that the parson was about to visit. Snuffy and Loweezy immediately forgot their quarrel and quickly clasped each other in loving embrace. As Jughaid opened the door, Loweezy sang out, "Howdy, Parson." The minister's visit symbolizes *the judgment* and we want to look good. But the judge is the object also of our negative feelings—though they remain hidden.

So we are torn by an internal tug-of-war between the

desire for a positive recognition from the judge and the desire to destroy his power. It is obvious that the judge is a tangible reminder of God. The "Hound of Heaven" can evoke both our fear and our hate. There are times when we would get rid of him if we could. Luther knew what it meant to feel this way. "For a heart completely cast down, and in despair," he said, "cannot open its mouth so wide, but it is dumb, or it slanders God and cannot think, believe, or speak of God other than as a fearful tyrant, or as of the Devil and only wants to flee and get away from him. Yes, it would that God were not God, so that he might not suffer such things from him."[1] Since God, whom we cannot get rid of, is "on our back," we feel constrained to make some sort of peace with Him—unless, of course, it is He who makes peace with *us*. With such projections coming between the minister and the people, it is a question of how much he functions as a pastor and how much as a symbol of moral coercion.

The Danger of Self-deception

These demands upon the minister may seem too much for his shaky self-confidence. In its survey of the Protestant minister, the *Saturday Evening Post* finds him saying, "Everytime ministers get together you hear over and over again the same cracked record—'I feel inadequate . . . inadequate . . . inadequate.' It's our theme song."[2] Charles Merrill Smith hams it up:

People expect their minister to be serious but not solemn; unworldly but possessed of some practical sense; wise but not smart; gentle but not effeminate; poor but not paupers; unctuous but not pompous; neat but not natty; diligent but not ambitious; upright in his own conduct but not censorious of theirs; forthright but tactful; affable but reserved.[3]

The frightening specter of his inner inadequacy can become too much of a threat and he may seek refuge in self-deception. Instead of looking within, where he has no control, he may concentrate instead on outer appearances, which he *can* control. Here is the basis for the development of a professional front that turns his vocation into role-playing. The leadership in faith with its credentials in the inner man is converted into a leadership with outer credentials. This leads to all sorts and conditions of legalism. Following the rules—the practices, the laws, the doctrines—becomes the frame upon which he rigidly constructs his leadership image.

He may become a legalist in morality or pietism and focus his spiritual leadership on being a watchdog on the conduct of the brethren. Or he may choose doctrine as his domain for leadership, and with all the rigidity of a moralist act as though having the correct intellectual formulations and proper word symbols makes the difference between the sheep and the goats. Or he may concentrate in the area of worship and become a legalist in matters of liturgics. The forms of worship then become the criterion for judgment, and the weightier matters are those of proper chancel apparel and symbolic gestures. He may even identify his leadership in faith with the espousal of liberal or conservative views on the social and political issues of the day, and justify his leadership by the passion with which he seeks "the Kingdom" through these causes.

All of these ways offer *something tangible* with which the minister can identify himself as a minister that will block out that *intangible something* with which he has difficulty identifying himself. Common to all of these ways is the implied self-justification offered in their endorsement in contrast to any justification by grace that would throw the focus on one's naked being. In each of them the minister is using "the cloth" to cover this nakedness. Since his identity as a person as well as a minister is tied up with the particular tangible credential, he espouses it with such authoritarian rigidity that he discourages any questioning either from within himself or from his people. The *show* must go on—

this holy masquerade, as Olov Hartmann calls it. The laymen's expectations that demand too much of the minister
constrain the insecure minister to demand too little from the
laymen. They need simply believe what he tells them. He
leads them into the same fraudulent security into which
the pressure to justify his authority has driven *him*.

Escape into Legalism

When the minister identifies his role with outer credentials, he uses his religion as an escape rather than as a solution to his inner problems. Instead of using the Gospel as the
basis for confronting himself, he uses it to bolster his front—
his professional defense system. Since it is a defense against
inner conflict, the energies of the conflict go into maintaining the defense. As we know from athletics, the best defense
is a good offense. Hence he may be tempted to attack those
who do not adhere to his particular legalism. The more he
can place the label of "wrong" on them, the more justified
he feels—for the more *wrong* these others are, the more
right he himself becomes. Thus his frustration is projected
onto this external conflict where right and wrong, good and
evil, truth and error engage in their struggle on a substitu-
tional level.

When he is engrossed in this manner with the maintenance of his professional defenses, the minister is left with
no time or opportunity to fluctuate in his moods as is the
layman. To face his inner deficiencies is too threatening
under this pressure to live a role. The tendency of the
theological student and the minister to have a low "d"—that
is, a low awareness of depression, or guilt—on his profile of
the Minnesota Multiphasic Personality Inventory could indicate that he tends to have underlying misgivings about
himself as a person. He may have confidence in his intellectual ability, his preaching or teaching ability or his administrative ability, but these do not substitute for his inner

selfhood where his leadership in faith centers. Here the self-image may be too threatening to look at directly without upsetting the balance maintained by his compensations and catapulting him into an acute sense of guilt or even despair.

The tyranny of the *should* about which the late cultural analyst Karen Horney speaks may exert a greater hold over the minister because of his leadership than over the layman. He may feel he cannot permit himself the normal ups and downs that characterize spiritual growth. Unlike physical growth, which is a more or less steady movement upward, spiritual growth follows a pattern of dips and rises, with the dip being the painful stimulus for the greater rise that follows. Progression is often preceded by regression. If, however, the minister finds it too threatening to his position of leadership in the faith to regress, how then can he experience any rise? If he cannot endure the dip, how can he progress? When he says "peace, peace" to himself when there is no peace, how long will it be before he is saying the same to others from the pulpit or in his pastoral care. Since this problem over self-worth is no different in kind in minister and layman, the layman may even encourage the minister in this questionable reassurance. We have a way of supporting each other in our defenses for our mutual protection.

Ministers associated with the renewal movement in the Church seek the opposite way of meeting the problem by attempting to break away from the cultural image of the ministry. As caricatured by Charles Merrill Smith, the cultural image is definitely pious but not necessarily religious. So the renewal clergy are determined not to be pious. Theirs is a "worldlier-than-thou" type of religious identity. Naturally, they tend to gravitate more to the ministries without a traditional pattern such as those in the missions of the inner city or in institutional chaplaincies rather than to the established parishes.

VII. THE LONELINESS OF THE MINISTRY

The more a person becomes aware of his individuality, the more he knows he is alone—cut off from others—facing sooner or later the most individual and lonely of all experiences—his own death. Religion is a confrontation with this loneliness. The soul yearns for intimacy. "As the hart panteth after the waterbrook, so panteth my soul after thee, O God." (Ps. 42:1) The religious experience is the experience of union with God in the "deep places of the soul." From this experience comes the hope that even death is penetrable. Union with God has the earmarks of a different order of being—an eternal order. Jesus said, "Lo, I am with you alway, even unto the end of the world." (Matt. 28:20)

The loneliness of individuality is not escaped through religion—in spite of the fact that some may attempt to misuse their religion for such a purpose. Rather the loneliness is transcended through religion. When Jesus said, "He that liveth and believeth in me shall never die," (John 11:26) He obviously did not mean that death could be avoided. He knew that He himself had to experience death. What He meant was that the soul in union with God could affirm life in the midst of death. The way of Christ is not that of denying the pain in life but of confronting it and triumphing over it. The soul's union with God is by faith—and faith is a leap—not away from the loneliness of life but through it. Jesus knew the loneliness of individuality in its most acute form when His disciples forsook Him and fled and even His heavenly Father seemed remote. Christ on His Cross is the symbol of rejection. Here He experienced the ultimate agony of loneliness—"My God, my God, why hast thou for-

saken me?" Yet in the midst of this extremity of estrange-
ment, He affirmed His intimacy with God—"Father, into thy
hands I commend my Spirit."

But this approach to the loneliness of life is difficult to
live out in the religious community. It leaves too many open
ends which we want to tack down. But when we do, we
box God in. If God could be boxed in, He would not be God
—and so our tacked-down religion is a religion without the
living God. The desire for a doubtproof religion is in reality
a rejection of faith.

The "Nice Prayer"

The challenge to allow God to be God is especially difficult for the leader in faith. The expectation is that he should
in a sense "capture" God. *His* convictions at least should be
doubt-free. That this is the implication of his role is shown
by his monopoly on prayer. As the expression of our relationship with God, prayer is our most concrete way of af-
firming God's presence. In most congregations the minister
is the official "prayerer." Many a congregational potluck
has been held up momentarily while someone located the
minister to "say grace." And who but the minister can give
the benediction at the community gathering, or give the
invocation at the father and son banquet of the Boy Scout
troop? It would seem to be the assumption that the minister has a "direct line" to God through which he can make
contact at a moment's notice.

In living up to this expectation the minister has to concentrate on the proper wording for his prayers. Like his
layman brother, he usually has a special vocabulary that he
reserves for God. Some also have a special voice in which
they pray, a "stained-glass voice" as it has been called—
characterized by a certain melodic lilt or quaver. Concentration is on the form, the voice, the phrase, even in the so-
called free prayer. I have frequently heard it said after the

invocation at a service club—"That was a *good* prayer," or
"a *nice* prayer." Our public prayers are politely worded and
abundant with thanksgivings and eulogies to the Deity.
Often they carry a punch line that contains a hidden or
unhidden moral.

This concern about wording is necessary in public prayer
—not because the leader is addressing God, but because he
is leading others in addressing God. While we may com-
municate with God in our inmost being with groanings that
cannot be uttered, we can hardly lead others without using
words that can be understood. The pressure is on the leader
to pray a *good* prayer.

But what we call good may not always be honest. Most
of us have some stored-up hostility toward God, or at least
toward providence, but our *good* prayers rarely express it.
It is rather difficult to express hostility in the carefully
chosen words and soothing tones of public prayer. Yet our
biblical heritage is something else. The prayers of the
prophets and even of the psalmists are not always *nice*
prayers. In fact, we hesitate to use some of them in our
public worship because of the hostility they express. Yet,
they are honest prayers.

The problem is that the minister's leadership pose in
prayer may carry over into his private prayer life. Here, of
course, it has no place. When the artificiality of it jars him
into serious reflection, the "direct line" is replaced by the
"unutterable groanings." As the illusion vanishes he knows
that he cannot box God in—even in a prayer pipeline—that
he cannot conjure up God's presence by simply striking the
prayer pose. He realizes again that there is no escape from
loneliness even as there is no substitute for faith. Rather
than facilitating his communication with God, the minister's leadership in prayer may become a barrier to this
communication.

This same barrier can extend also to the minister's communication with people. As with all leadership roles, his

position is a strain on natural communication. The president of the company can never be sure that his relationship with his staff is on the level of honest communication. They are more concerned about pleasing him because of his position than because of his person. When he has to make the decisions that affect the future of the company, he knows also the loneliness of responsibility. Yet, the minister may be even more conscious of his isolation because his leadership centers in the inner life. As he attempts to penetrate the loneliness of others, he may actually increase his own sense of loneliness. The ministry is a lonely vocation.

The wife feels the loneliness even more than the minister. The ministry is his vocation, and his professional challenge takes up much of the void. Some ministers' wives make their husbands' ministry their vocations also. For them, too, the vocation helps to fill the vacuum. But the majority of ministers' wives are first of all wives and mothers. They are more than *pastors'* wives; they are persons with needs like all other persons. The minister's wife is a symbol of the lonely crowd as she involves herself with many people, but with little mutuality of sharing. The parish is her exile from intimate friendships.

The Lack of Real Friends

With whom shall the minister and his wife be friends? Naturally, they are friends with the members of the congregation. By this we mean that they are friendly with them and may even know some of them intimately. Yet, this is not friendship in the sense of mutuality and preferential companionship. The very nature of the role of the pastor and his wife to the members of the congregation limits the extent to which they can be friends. Whether he wants to be, or even whether he should be, in this unique position in the congregation, the fact remains that he *is*. He is the leader, the authority figure, the VIP of the parish, and his wife shares in this status. There are those who are attracted to him on this basis. They want to be in on the inner circle. Jesus also had this trouble. He had His inner circle—Peter, James, and John—whom He chose from among the twelve to accompany Him on special occasions. The quarreling of the disciples over who was the greatest might have been influenced by this. At least, when the mother of James and John asked for special positions for her sons in Jesus' coming kingdom, the others were incensed.

Yet, even when there is no inner circle, people may assume there is one—and want to be in it. Others may feel just the opposite. They are repelled by this "sucking" of authority and fight the practice by fighting the pastor. Perhaps they simply feel unable to compete and so they attack. Apparently they find it emotionally intolerable to lower their guard for fear of being "taken in." Or perhaps they view the pastor as a rival to their own aspirations for authority.

If the pastor and his wife form their intimate friendships within the congregation, they are jeopardizing his pastoral role with these people. In defending his friendships with specific couples within the congregation, a minister pointed to the fact that when one of the group had surgery, he was able to minister to him without any barrier. "Yes," replied another minister, "but what if it had been a marriage crisis rather than surgery?" He had a point—particularly since family crises constitute the largest demand upon the pastoral ministry.

The couple who are intimate friends of the pastor and his wife may be reluctant to involve the pastor in their domestic problems simply because he is too close to them. They sense intuitively that their friendship has reduced his pastoral potential. Even if they should contact him about their problems, what would happen then to their friendship? From their differentiated roles in the counseling process, could they return to the mutuality of intimate friendship?

Perhaps it is to preserve the friendship as a friendship that they choose not to risk involving him pastorally. The pastoral role in itself, however, is structured to endure the strains of catharsis—providing it does not have to carry the weight of other responsibilities in addition.

The pastor as a person has the need for people for whom he has no unique responsibility, nor they to him, and with whom he can develop mutual friendships. The same is true for his wife. Other ministers and their wives offer the best potential for these friendships. Their common education, vocation, and concerns naturally predispose them to mutuality. However, there are also obstacles. Ministers can feel competitive toward each other, particularly when their congregations are striving for similar community recognition. Also the potential busyness of the ministry offers the minister a substitute for friendships if he is so inclined. Consequently, though they have common interests, some ministers and their wives may not respond to the overtures from their colleagues. They may not return the invitations, and the potential friendship fails to develop because the interest is one-sided. The frequent moving of ministers is another obstacle to friendship. In my own community, for example, there is only one minister who was here ten years ago. The majority have tenures of less than three years. Consequently, friendships between parsonages may be short-lived.

There are of course other possibilities. Since the minister is a professional person, he has potential friends in other professional people. Yet, until recently the minister has been on the bottom of the professional totem pole—or at least he has so thought of himself. His sense of professional inferiority has prevented him and his wife from taking much initiative in this direction. Probably to others they seem aloof.

Laymen of other churches constitute another source for friendships. The problem is that most laymen are not accustomed to having clergymen as intimate friends. They may shy away from it until the initial mental block is broken down. Often neighbors are the most logical laymen friends. After expressing his appreciation for the friendship he and his wife had developed with the couple next door, a minister voiced his apprehension. "They're talking about joining my church. For the sake of our friendship, I'm just hoping they won't."

Isolated in the Midst of People

Because of these obstacles in developing mutual friends, the minister and his wife may find themselves emotionally isolated in the midst of people. As a minister he is concerned about the needs of others and offers to meet these needs. But what about his own needs—and his wife's needs? In his preaching and pastoral care he is giving himself emotionally all of the time. But what about his opportunities for emotional restoration? The minister is the opposite of the sponge in that he is squeezing it all out but not soaking it back up. It may be argued that he is receiving while he is giving—that it is through giving that we receive. Yet, this is not the emotional re-creation to which we are referring. For this he needs the relaxed atmosphere of intimate fellowship in which his *purpose* is to receive as well as to give.

It may also be argued that, while the minister may lack the intimacy of close friendships, he has as compensation the intimate fellowship of God. Yet, God never meant Himself to be a substitute for people. In fact, the interpersonal isolation in which the pastor may find himself can obstruct his relationship with God. This obstruction may occur even when he is supposedly in the act of fellowship with others if maintaining his role inhibits his spontaneity. The God we know through Christ is an incarnate God. The Church is His body and the fellowship of the Church mediates the fellowship with His Spirit.

Unfortunately this fellowship may be experienced more outside of the organized group life of the congregation than within it because of the pattern of conformity that often characterizes organized fellowship. Regardless of where it occurs we all need this fellowship—including the pastor and his wife. The minister's work can substitute temporarily for this fellowship. For some this substitution may become a lifetime habit—but at the cost of being genuine persons. Such an individual can relate to others only on the basis of meeting their needs, and he is unable to recognize that he too has needs—specifically for others as persons.

It's Hardest on the Wife

The loneliness of the ministry in the rural areas and small towns is worse than in the cities. Because of the limitations of these communities, there is less potential outside of the congregation for intimate friendships. Also the patterns for relating socially are more set. Often the minister and his wife are not considered for the various social groupings of the community. These patterns have a community history and the history is accepted uncritically. It would surprise many that the minister and his wife would even want to branch out socially. It is assumed that they have their place within the social framework of the church organizations. This isolation is particularly hard on the wife. She probably came into the community with her husband directly from the seminary community where she likely enjoyed the intimate fellowship of the seminary trailer court or married-student apartment. The change is difficult to take.

The small towns are feeling the decline in the rural areas most acutely. Increasingly they are possessing more of a past than a future. The majority of the young people leave to go to the larger cities. Those that remain become infected with the deteriorating morale of the community. "It's hard to fight it," said a spirited wife of a town church. "I'm afraid

if we stay here long I'll become as unimaginative as everybody else seems to be." I happen to know at the moment
several young ministers who are seriously considering leaving the ministry if they are not placed in more challenging
parishes. In each instance the wife is unhappy because she is
lonely.

A man—even a minister—can be very partisan when it
comes to his wife, and this defensiveness adds to the problem. Not every young woman who falls in love with a
theological student feels as called to the life of the ministry
as does her sweetheart. Sometimes she has had to have a
great deal of reassuring before she has been ready to take
the step. If now she is unhappy because she is lonely, her
husband feels somewhat responsible. When people marry,
they become one flesh, and as a consequence they com-
pound each other's isolation or feelings of being abused. The
minister may find it hard not to resent the congregation and
the community that leaves his wife feeling left out. Although he could occupy himself with his work, he feels
his loneliness all the more because of her. "We are deeply
lonely people," said a small-town pastor. "Particularly my
wife is extremely lonesome, and I can see why. We live in
an emotional and intellectual vacuum. I thought that if I
ministered to the needs of the congregation, they would in
turn minister to the needs of my family. This has proved
unrealistic." Their marriage, like any other marriage, needs
the company of other couples for its own healthy development. Otherwise, they begin to drain each other's emotional reserve.

The Congregation Should Understand

The minister needs to place this issue of friendship on his
priority list. Some may question this. Walter Wagoner,
for example, says, "The office of the ordained ministry does
properly entail a dignity, a visibility, an aloneness. One of

the hallmarks of faithfulness in the ministry is the willingness to endure this aspect of professionalization. With humor, with perspective and with good grace, it can be done."[1] Of course it can! But is there any need in making the vocation more lonely than it is by its very nature? Much of this loneliness could be alleviated. There is no particular virtue in enduring unnecessary privation.

The congregation should understand this need of the pastor and his wife for friends and not feel deprived when they establish such friendships or be offended by their privacy in these matters. Even when they select their friends from within the congregation—and others deem this to be unwise, and perhaps rightly so—the layman can best serve the cause of the ministry by being understanding. In some communities the congregation may provide the minister and his wife with the only realistic opportunity for friends, and if the choice is between establishing intimate friendships within the congregation or being unhappy and lonely, the former is surely the lesser of the two evils.

The minister and his wife need offer no apology for having special friends or preferred groups. Their selection is no violation of democracy. The issue rather is *philia* or friendship love, which is by its very nature selective and preferential. The need for friends is a very human need—like the need for recreation. There is nothing distinctly Christian about it except that the Christian life is lived within the human life. As the German pastor Christoph Blumhart put it, "The human being first must become a Christian, and then the Christian must again become a human being." Christ takes us out of the world and then puts us back again. Like other human experiences, friendship is incorporated or *baptized* into the Christian life. It then becomes a friendship within the fellowship. *Philia* love helps to satisfy the pastor's needs as a human being so that he can offer *agape* love to all.

The Need for a Father Confessor

The minister has a need also for intimacy in the pastoral sense—the opportunity for a father confessor, an opportunity that he offers to others. This need was envisaged in the office of the bishop or district president who serves as a pastor to pastors. However, the bishop or his equivalent is also the pastor's superior in the hierarchy of the ordained ministry. Naturally the pastor is going to think twice before saying anything to him that may damage this superior's image of him. Even if such matters as a future position did not enter his mind, the minister shares in the natural desire for approval from the authority.

An additional obstacle to the bishop's functioning as a pastor to pastors is his involvement with administrative duties. In our administratively oriented age he may possibly have been chosen for his position more because of his administrative rather than his pastoral ability. The territory which he administers is often geographically large and presents limitations to his pastoral potential. Unlike other functions of the ministry, the counseling ministry has a need rather than a time schedule. A father confessor a hundred miles away is hardly available for something as unscheduled as immediate needs.

The most likely father confessors are fellow pastors. Here, however, the minister runs into the problem that these men are often his peers, even in age, and also at times his competitors. These are men in the same vocation, working in the same community, and often involved in the same problems. Men are reluctant to admit that they need help and even more reluctant to ask for it. The same sense of failure that other men experience when they ask for *his* help, the minister himself experiences when he seeks help for himself or his family. Of the marital catastrophes in the parsonage of which I am aware, the problem existed long before it became public knowledge. Yet, in only one of these in-

stances did the minister or his wife seek any help before-
hand. The minister partakes of the masculine defensiveness
of our culture. Let's face it—big boys don't cry!

Yet, whenever ministers are provided with counseling
help without the usual complications, the response is large.
Obviously he desires this opportunity, providing it does
not jeopardize his position. Even in the local conferences,
when ministers gather together, one may unburden himself
to another with a modicum of encouragement. Commenting on this situation, a minister said, "After the guy gets
through bending your ear with all of his troubles, you almost feel as though you should tell him *yours*—to keep
things on a par." He was voicing the tension that occurs
when one finds himself in a counseling relationship with
one of his peers. This tension is eased considerably when
there is a significant age or experience span between the
"counselor" and the "counselee." Some localities are discovering that counseling opportunities made available to ministers by church-related clinical centers offer the most
satisfactory answer to the problem. The Methodist Church
in some of its areas such as Indiana and Ohio has established
counseling services for its pastors. In one of the districts of
the American Lutheran Church there is an official pastoral
counselor to pastors. In each of these situations the important factor is that the counselor is not expected to report
to anybody, especially to the bishop or district president.

There are times when the minister may need the help
of another professional—the psychiatrist or the psychologist.
Contrary to what some may feel under these circumstances,
there need be no sense of failure in securing this help. In
fact, the greater judgment rests on the minister who is too
proud—or frightened—to seek it. The idea inherent in the
structure of the Church is that God works through human
beings to help human beings. The function of ministry is
not limited to the ordained clergy. In the language of
Luther each believer is a "little Christ" to his neighbor. It

is to *each* other and not specifically to an *ordained* other that St. James says we should confess our sins that we may be healed. Nor is the influence of God limited to the lives of believers. God can use even the atheist to carry out His will. He can work through the psychiatrist—even the non-Christian psychiatrist—to help the Christian minister with his emotional problems so that he can be restored to a more effective ministry.

The Value of Group Meetings

Recently I visited an old seminary friend and was impressed by his openness and honesty. I knew he had not always possessed these qualities and so I asked him about it. "For the last five years," he said, "a group of us pastors has been meeting each week for breakfast. During this time we have grown to trust each other and the sharing in this group has been the greatest thing to happen for my ministry." In recent years there have been more and more of these sharing groups among ministers in which problems can be aired in the milieu of intimate fellowship. We have such groups for our seminary students, who find them very valuable for their growth in self-awareness. Besides helping him to meet his personal needs, the group provides the pastor with the experience he needs to establish a similar intimacy in the fellowship life of his congregation.

The potential for a ministers' group varies with the community, but if the group cuts across denominational lines there are likely to be enough interested clergymen to begin. It is best if the group has a leader—an experienced pastor, a chaplain supervisor from an area institution, or even a psychiatrist or clinical psychologist. Though ministers tend to move frequently, it is advisable not to add to the group or replace those who leave until the group reconvenes after a summer recess. In this way it can achieve a certain identity before it completes its natural cycle. Some groups are made up of ministers and their wives in order to provide the wife with the same opportunity and to focus on the marital relationship in terms of parsonage tensions. Groups for wives alone are also a possibility, particularly when they are structured along the lines of a study or interest group.[2]

VIII. CONFLICTS OVER THE DEVOTIONAL LIFE

The occasional need for a fellow pastor or some other professional counselor assists the pastor in his counseling relationship with God and does not substitute for it. The real need is to share our inner life with God. If we can bare to Him our fears, our inadequacies, our doubts, our guilts, our resentments, and our discouragements, not only is there no need for a front, but the essential meaning of the Gospel as acceptance by grace is functionally understood. Such a connection with God is a source of stability for the minister during this period of crisis. As Walter Wagoner put it, "There are few experiences so revealing of the future staying power and growth of a parish minister as his habits of worship and devotion."[1] Through his personal prayer life the minister sustains in his own mind his identity as a minister—and as a person. It is his meaningful relationship to the Master that gives to the disciple his sense of identity—of calling.

The Master Himself went through His own crisis of identity in the Garden of Gethsemane when the darkening events pointed to the cross. Out of the agony of bloody sweat, he prayed, "Father, if thou art willing, remove this cup from me." Yet it was for this cause that He had come. In his temporary confusion He prayed intently, "Nevertheless, not my will, but thine, be done." (Luke 22:41–44) Arising from that struggle for identity in which He wrestled like Jacob with God, he was able to face Judas and the soldiers, strengthened and confirmed in his Messianic commitment.

His great disciple Paul experienced nothing but frustration during his second missionary journey when he had no clear sense of direction concerning where he was to go. He was conscious only that the Holy Spirit was blocking his every intention. Yet this very awareness meant that he was conscious of divine purpose even in his frustration. Because of this consciousness he was open to the revelation by night that he was to go over into Macedonia—thus making the historic step onto European soil.

Yet, the minister may have his conflicts over the devotional life. Obviously if it were the staying power for which it has the potential, the crisis today would not be as threatening to the minister's identity. We have seen that, when the pastor develops a professional front, he may find it difficult to dispense with this front when he prays. His public prayers are part of his professional activity and for this the front is no problem. But when he attempts to pray privately, these artificialities seem out of place—and even repulsive. Here the façade must come down, and rather than praying nicely, he must pray honestly.

There are also other conflicts over his devotional life and these he shares with the layman. I find that it is usually an embarrassing question when I ask a person about his prayer life. "Well, it's not what it should be," is the usual response. Consequently, layman and minister can explore this conflict together, since it is of common concern.

There Is No Time

The most obvious difficulty with one's devotional life is in finding the time for it. The minister's schedule is not conducive to devotional hours. The traditional devotional times are before retiring in the evening or upon arising in the morning. The minister's evenings are usually taken up with pastoral work and meetings. By the time he is ready for bed he may be too tired to do much more than read a brief scripture and say a brief prayer. Getting to bed late at night is not conducive to getting up early in the morning. By the time he gets out of bed, shaves, and has his breakfast, it is time for him to be at his study or office. Once there, the ringing of the telephone and other administrative matters make it clear that he has to "get down to work."

The problem, however, goes deeper. The devotional life does not fit into our noncontemplative culture. The monk at his prayers is not harassed by such things as telephones or family responsibilities or home appliances that need fixing. Besides, his prayers are considered part of his work. But the minister is caught up in a production-centered culture, and his devotional life is more likely to put him behind in his work than be considered part of it. Consequently, the difficulty in finding the time for a devotional life is a symptom rather than the cause of the conflict over it.

Against the Grain of Our Culture

We tend to have our problems over things that are difficult for us. Behind the problem over devotions there is a double-mindedness toward devotions. We feel we should have a devotional life and at the same time we resist it. What is there about the devotional life that we should resist? If we examine it we find that it runs against our cultural grain in at least three ways. First, the devotional life is a reflective activity—that is, it throws us into ourselves. Most of us feel uncomfortable when we stop to think about ourselves and our purpose for living. Normally we prefer to be distracted about this time. Secondly, the devotional life has the appearance of inactivity. Nothing tangible is being produced—no work is being done. We are an activist society and are concerned primarily about getting things accomplished. Thirdly, the devotional life confronts us with intimacy with God. Many of us feel ill at ease in such intimacy—it brings us closer to God than we care to get. We feel more secure in *doing* than in *being*. Intimacy with God or with our neighbor challenges our sense of worth as persons—apart from our accomplishments. It exposes us to exposure.

In the whirling mind of today's activist, the lurking anxiety about his destiny, his purpose for being, and his inadequacy as a person can seemingly be allayed only by *doing*—and more *doing*. Despite the Church's emphasis on justification by grace, our society is held together with justification by works. When one is *doing*, he is working to keep things under control. When he is not doing, he is leaving himself open to his own fears. Some people drink rather than work to prevent this exposure, but the motivation is the same.

The fear of the unpredictable—the unknown—raises its specter even in our *doing*. Most ministers are more at ease in speaking than in listening. The emphasis on preaching in the ministry leads them in this direction. They are better at delivering a sermon or teaching a lesson than they are at conducting a discussion. Listening and discussing involve us dynamically with others. One of the characteristics of any dynamic situation is that it is unpredictable. So in spite of the teacher's good and even announced intentions to "leave time for discussion," he rarely does. And if he does, he consumes it by a long-winded answer to the first question. So long as we are talking (doing), we have things under control. Most of us fear the unstructured moment.

The Protestant world does not place much value upon meditation. From a functional point of view it seems a waste of valuable time. To those who wish to meditate, we give our blessing—so long as their numbers are small. We can take a few oddballs in any crowd. They receive our awe but not our emulation. Meditation is a symbol for the superfluous.

The busiest of our ministerial activists are our home missionaries. Because they are subsidized by the denominational headquarters they "punch the clock" on a number of matters, including the number of calls they make per month. It can be discouraging work when the activist formula does not produce results. One such discouraged missionary decided to quit making calls and to spend his time in prayer and meditation. Naturally this was looked upon as a sign of mental deterioration—perhaps it was. At least it was an example of extremism. However, from a biblical point of view the usual activism is also an extreme. Yet, we accept this extreme and reject the meditative extreme.

The Fear of Being Superfluous

Ironically, if the meditative aspect of the minister's work is of questionable importance, his profession itself is of questionable importance—for the ministry is grounded on the superfluous. As far as our production is concerned, the minister would contribute more if he put his shoulder to the wheel of industry. Although most of us would acknowledge that Jesus had a point when He said that man does not live by bread alone, the fact remains that most of us are also going all out for bread. Therefore, a vocation devoted to something which is not bread is somewhat of a luxury—something nice to have if you can afford it.

Sensing that some view him as superfluous, the minister may try in one way or another to prove he is essential. Perhaps our contemporary emphasis on administration in the Church is an unconscious attempt to adorn the ministry with the mantle of economic necessity. At least the ministry can thus shed the *format* of the superfluous. But if the superfluous turns out to be the essential, the adaptation to cultural values could be a loss. How hard it is for the church administrator to be caught up to the third heaven! Even if his production orientation were open to visions and revelations, it is doubtful if he would have the time.

If the minister needs the human dialogue to sustain himself in the current ministerial crisis, how much more does he need the dialogue with the divine in, with, and beyond the human. The basis for a counseling relationship with God is in a disciplined devotional life. One's dialogue with people is also devotional in nature—providing his life has a devotional orientation. Our dialogue with God and our dialogue with people must complement each other before they can unite with each other. Without a complementary dialogue with people, our dialogue with God is prone to degenerate into a dialogue with ourselves. As Jesus said, "The Pharisee stood and prayed thus *with himself.*" (Luke 18:11) If people are viewed simply as means to an end—that is, as symbols of our obligation to God—they cease to be people and our fellowship ceases to be a fellowship.

By the same token, without a complementary dialogue with God, our dialogue with people tends to lose its mediating or sacramental dimension and become a pale-blooded imitation of its potential. God can neither be separate from the human fellowship nor identical with it. The biblical analogy for this relationship between God and His people is the relationship of marriage. One does not lose his individuality when he becomes married, but at the same time his individuality cannot be viewed apart from his marriage. Before either partner in a marriage can become *one flesh* with the other, they must become persons in their own right. Before they can become the *means* for a union, they must be *ends* in themselves.

Can the Leader of Worship Also Worship?

This same complementation applies also to corporate worship. In this milieu we would expect that the union of the divine and the human would be most obvious. Yet, the role of the leader in worship is somewhat different from the role of the participant. The leader concentrates upon involving the participant. Conscious of the fact that he stands out from the others, he cannot—yea, dare not—lose himself in the worship experience. If his prayers begin to sound like sermons or the reading of the service like rhetoric, it is because he is both out of it and in it so far as his own worship is concerned.

The young minister, particularly, can have as many nightmares over losing his place in the order of worship as losing his notes in the delivery of the sermon. Most of our Protestant church services are "one-man shows." The only break the congregation gets from "beholding the minister" is during the singing of the congregation or the choir and when the collection is taken. Therefore, as much as the minister may dislike the idea, the conception of the service as well as the sermon as a *performance* constantly reoccurs. I can recall from my own seminary days that those students who had excelled in speech or dramatics at college were likely to give a good account of themselves as preachers and as leaders in worship because of their disciplined control of voice and countenance for purposes of communication. This is no reflection upon their sincerity, but is rather a confirmation of the kinship between these communication skills and leadership in worship.

What then is the cumulative effect upon one who is involved as a leader in worship as differentiated from a participant in worship? A minister who has only one service on Sunday morning makes it a practice to attend an early service in a neighboring congregation. "I find it helpful to my spiritual life as well as to my ministry to involve myself in a service for which I have no responsibility," he says. Perhaps this combination of leader and participant offers the best balance.

When a minister for one reason or another—and the opportunities are becoming more and more numerous—leaves the parish ministry for a nonparish ministry, he is rarely content with his resumed participant status in worship. Instead, he is more likely to be critical of the way the leader conducts the service and of the sermons he preaches.

While he may be justified in his criticisms, one wonders if he has not lost the touch for participation. He is too used to "running the show" to be "caught up" in it.

Thus not even corporate worship is beyond the danger of this divorce between the divine and the human. In our public worship as in our other fellowship activities, it is our own prayer life that helps preserve the divine dimension in our perspective. The marriage of the divine and the human makes human activities religious, but it is our own involvement in this marriage that makes these activities religious for *us*.

With Earnest Desire, There Will Be Time

The pastor needs to recognize the ambivalence in his frequent lament that he cannot find the time for a disciplined devotional life. He needs to do the same with his other lament that he cannot find the time for calling. What we consistently put off due to the press of other demands, we either value lightly or are resisting. While it seems to one that he is a prisoner in these matters, the fact remains that the prisoner may be in love with his chains.

Jesus' parable of the two sons who were told by their father to work in the vineyard (Matt. 21:28–32) gives us an insight into why we may fail to live up to our intentions. The son who said, "I go, sir," was desirous to please. But somehow he never got around to fulfilling his intention. The other son who said, "I will not," was openly defiant. Yet, it was he who afterward went to the vineyard. Obviously the son who faced his resistance was able to cope with it. As Jesus said, "He repented." Beneath the conscious "I will" is the subconscious "I will not." But how can one honestly repent until the subconscious becomes conscious? And how can he reverse things to "go to the vineyard" unless he repents?

To present oneself as a victim of circumstances in these omissions is to be guilty of what Kierkegaard calls "altering the conception of what earnestness is."[2] When we substitute being troubled for being repentant, we distort the meaning of earnestness. One of the marks of a sincere confession is the determination to do better. This determination may be unsupported by our feelings. It may have to affirm itself as an act of our naked will. It may also have to cut through all the fog and confusion that says we cannot act now. When this determination reckons with the reality that the *fifth column* is within, it is less likely to be sidetracked.

The story is told of a toad who fell into a rut in the road and could not seem to hop out. He called to a passing toad to assist him. "If I help you," said the toad, "I may fall into the rut with you. Then there would simply be two of us who are trapped." So he hopped on. Later to his surprise he saw the trapped toad hopping down the road. "I thought you couldn't get out of that rut," he said. "I couldn't," said the toad, "but a big truck came along and I had to!"

It is amazing what we can do when we are determined to do it. It is equally amazing how little we can do when we are ambivalent. Then we confine ourselves to such matters as interpretation and problems of interpretation as substitutes for action. As described in the book of Acts, the early Church had a strong awareness of the guidance of the Holy Spirit and a penchant for prayer and fasting. This is no coincidence, for the two go together. The decision to send Paul and Barnabas on their historic missionary enterprise—a decision which has given us about half of our New Testament in Paul's missionary letters—came about when the prophets and teachers at Antioch—Barnabas, Symeon, Lucius, Manaen, and Paul—were worshiping the Lord and fasting. It was then that the Holy Spirit said, "Set apart for me Barnabas and Saul for the work that I have called them." Again it was "after fasting and prayer" that "they laid their hands on them and sent them off." (Acts 13:1–3)

Fasting is a lost practice in our churches. Its abuse has led to its disuse rather than its proper use. And prayer is fighting for its life at the edge of an administratively minded Church concerned with efficiency of operation and getting the results. But what of our awareness of the Spirit's guidance? Instead we have a crisis in the ministry and "psychological hand wringing," which Walter Wagoner calls a "typical Protestant substitute for prayer and fasting."[3]

The Example of Jesus

The devotional life of Jesus is an example both to the minister and to the layman. In the beginning of Jesus' ministry Mark notes that "in the morning, a great while before day, he rose and went out to a lonely place and prayed." (Mark 1:35) As His ministry progressed Luke states that "in these days he went out into the hills to pray; and all night he continued in prayer to God." (Luke 6:12) It was after He had taken with Him Peter, James, and John and climbed a mountain specifically to pray that He experienced His transfiguration. (Luke 9:28) As His ministry came to its climax, Judas knew where Jesus could be found because He went out "as was his custom" to the Mount of Olives in the evening to pray. (Luke 22:39)

We will have to admit that Jesus' example in prayer is a little strenuous. Yet, there is value in the custom of having regular times for prayer. One of these should be the first thing in the morning. Getting the proper orientation at the beginning of the day has its good influence on what follows and is worth far more even to our health than the extra half hour we could stay in bed. Another time is prior to the supper hour. For this we have a precedent in the life of St. Peter. His prayer life is more adaptable to our lives than that of Jesus. In fact, he even went to sleep saying his prayers—and this should really help us to identify with him.

It was while he was visiting in the home of Simon the

Tanner at Joppa that he went up on the housetop to pray about six o'clock in the evening. This is the time of day when a man gets hungry, and while supper was being prepared below, Peter fell into a trancelike sleep and began to dream about food. As the decision to send Paul and Barnabas as missionaries to the Gentiles came out of prayer and fasting, so Peter's decision to break with his Jewish tradition and enter the home of a Gentile came out of this prayer experience. Although the food he saw in the vision was unclean to a Jew, the voice from heaven bade him eat. When the messengers from the Roman centurion Cornelius arrived to request that Peter accompany them to tell the Gospel to Cornelius, Peter interpreted the vision as God's direction to go.

The time prior to the supper hour is of distinct advantage for the pastor or any man whose work consumes a great deal of emotional energy—even as it is obviously not the best time for the housewife. A break for rest and meditation and committing the day's events to God at this time makes it possible for the pastor to join the family circle with a refreshed spirit. Otherwise he may be with his family in the body while his mind belabors the problems of the day. The minister who attempts to join himself to his family table directly from his work involvement is exposing his stomach to indigestion and the family atmosphere to tension. Even if he should fall asleep in his presupper withdrawal, he would not only be in good company, but would be giving evidence to the relaxing influence of prayer.

The pastor's devotional life, like that of the layman, is his counseling relationship with God. Combining the openness to receive that characterizes meditation with the cathartic expression of confession, the minister may clear the confusion from his mind regarding his commitment. The feeling of being lost that he at times has, which he cannot express as a leader in prayer, he can express in his room when he has shut the door. Here the feelings that need to come out can

come out. Those to whom they directly refer may not understand. Therefore, it is not always wise to tell them. God,
who sees the inner as well as the outer, *does* understand. We
can express these tensions to our Father who is in secret and
receive our release. At these secret times we have more
affinity for the fierce language of some of the psalms than
we do in our public services.

In his devotional life the pastor can get his thinking
straight concerning what *can* be done and what *cannot*.
Through his relationship with God, which is exercised by
this experience, he receives the courage to do what needs to
be done and the confidence to commit to God what he cannot do. This is the value of a *pastoral* counseling relationship. It is therefore one of the benefits from a counseling
relationship with God. From these times of prayer, which
may in one instance reflect the storm of Gethsemane and
in another the tranquility of the Joppa rooftop, the pastor
more often than not finds himself refreshed in spirit and
restored emotionally.

Persistency Is Needed

Any devotional life has its dry periods when one derives
no obvious benefit from it and subsequently loses all desire
to continue. Contrary to our feelings, this is the time for
persistence in prayer rather than for giving up. "What shall
I pray when I feel nothing?" we may ask. We can express
to God the very dearth that is disturbing us. Dryness in the
devotional life is a symptom of the problem. Since it is
emotional in nature, it too shall pass, for if there is one con-
stancy to our emotions, it is their constant fluctuation. We
do not feel like talking when we are depressed either, but
it is the best thing to do, regardless. The important thing
about prayer is that we share what *is*—our present concern.
When we share our present concern—whatever is uppermost
in our mind at the present moment—the dialogue of the

devotional is at a pertinent level, for we are sharing ourselves.

This same persistence is also necessary for our family devotions. There are times when most of us wonder why we bother with family devotions. Simply to take the time for it may create dissension. The children may seem bored and the devotional material unrelated to anyone's concerns. It is then that we may recall Paul's words, "Let us not grow weary in well doing, for in due season we shall reap, if we do not lose heart." (Gal. 6:9) Yet, we may honestly question whether our attempts at family devotions are really "well doing." Having been reared in a home with daily family devotions and having continued the practice with my present family, I definitely believe it is "well doing." The dry periods when the practice seems meaningless are a challenge to us to vary the procedure and give more thought to the material. The same challenge to do something different occurs when we experience a dearth in our personal devotions.

Family devotions become a meaningful family tradition for those families who persist despite all the obvious reasons for giving it up. This period in the day can develop into the one time when the family has a discussion together. Often this discussion takes off spontaneously from the devotion —which may never be finished as it was planned. This discussion usually comes when the children reach high school age. Much of the rebellion of these years, even against religion, may be wholesomely though vehemently expressed at these times. Parents who can listen as well as talk—who can ask questions about which they are concerned as well as answer them—can learn much about their children and *from* them. This may be particularly difficult for the minister and his wife since they may feel defensive about having rebels in the ranks, and carry over their role as religious authorities into the family circle. Yet, with persistence they, too, can learn to relax in the midst of heresy and attacks on conventional morality.

The family devotional has its carry-over into the life of the family, though it is not always perceptible. Even adults may profit from what they do not appreciate at the time —and children much more so. They would miss the practice if it were dropped, even though they approach it at times as though they "couldn't care less." Family traditions add to the cohesiveness of the family, and when these traditions are religious they add the vertical dimension to this cohesiveness that gives a deeper sense of security to the child.

We are obsessed today by the profit motive. "What do we get out of it?" Or its reverse, "I don't seem to be getting anything out of it." This uncritical assumption of the economic spirit into our religious life needs to be challenged. It is the product of an efficiency expert mentality which has to *see* the results. Challenging the old forms is good and needs to be done continually. But there is the possibility of an escape motive whenever we dispense with what is difficult—and especially when we justify it on the basis of results. Ours is the need to be doing—the compulsion to latch on to the tangible. Because the devotional life is not a *doing* activity or even a tangible activity, we have difficulty justifying the time that we would give it. Yet, the fact remains that if we are to pray without ceasing, as the apostle suggests, there must be those times when we cease all in order to pray.

IX. THE STRUGGLE FOR TIME

The American Church is known for its stewardship emphasis. We send our experts to the mother churches in Europe
to teach them how we do it. This American know-how is
concentrated in the three familiar areas—time, talents, and
possessions (a better word than money). While the most
important of these for the stewardship program is possessions—raising the budget—the most complicated of the three
for the stewardship *life* is time.

There are occasions when time is more precious to us than
money. We even speak about "buying time," as though we
were trading money for it. We also refer to the misuse of
time as wasting time, with the same implied judgment that
goes with wasting money. There are also occasions when
we would be only too happy to give our time away if we
could—just to be rid of it. "My, didn't the time pass quickly,"
says the bored traveler with obvious relief after a pleasant
conversation with a fellow passenger. The same individual
may find himself lamenting in the not too distant future, "If
I only had more time!"

Our complicated approach to time is an example of the
paradox—the dialectic—in life. On the one hand we cannot
seem to get enough of it, and on the other we wish it were
over. Time *flies*—our fastest speed; it also drags. We covet it,
and we are bored with it. We lament the speed with which
time passes and yet we can hardly wait until it does. We
enjoy it and are frightened of it. We struggle for it in order
to get things done, and if we should obtain an extra allot-
ment, we might get panicky over what to do with it. Right
now I am in a struggle for time to write this chapter, and yet

if I were suddenly given an unexpected boon in time, my efficiency would probably decrease. We live in the midst of the busiest society on earth and yet the typical American spends five hours and twenty-five minutes a day—1977 hours a year—watching television.[1]

We do better with anticipated time than with present time. Our good intentions and optimistic plans belong to the future and are often in contrast to our present inefficiency. Yet, these visions and dreams are necessary or we lose our incentive even to live. They help us to muddle through the less dramatic here and now. It is particularly tragic when a minister loses his vision. When he can see no future to his work, he loses interest in the present. There may be much that he could do, but he has no incentive. So he tries to do what little has to be done but he ends up not even doing that. As the song has it—you have to have a dream to make a dream come true.

The Overly Busy Man

Time, like money, may also be tied up with our identity. The overly burdened minister may be a man who is compulsively busy. Timewise he has a need to be strapped. He is less conscious of this need, however, than the pastor who feels it necessary to look busy even when he is not. Yet the need is the same—it is the need to prove. But to prove what? Probably that his work is important—necessary—that he is not a superfluous shaman. The fact that his work is less structured than most jobs adds to his uneasiness in this respect. Also his "hours" are differently proportioned than the majority of the work force.

Although he has to smile good-naturedly, the minister gets awfully tired of hearing the old josh, "You preachers have it easy—all you got to do is get ready for Sunday." He knows, of course, that people do not really believe this. Yet, the jest points out that the one inflexible time in his schedule is Sunday morning. The fact that thousands of clergymen traveled from all sections of the country for civil rights demonstrations is evidence not only of the unique concern of the clergy but of the unique adjustability of the clergyman's time. What layman has so flexible a work schedule?

Judging by any fair evaluation, the demands upon the minister's time are unending. There are exceptions of course. Some congregations are so limited by their own geography that they offer little challenge beyond a "custodial care" type of ministry. Fortunately the progress of the ecumenical movement is making possible the merger of some of these limited congregations to form more challenging parishes. Also a minister may overstay his ministry in a particular congregation and fall victim to vocational lethargy. While a change of environment is rarely the sole answer for anyone's problems, it is amazing how much "the right move" can mean to the resurgence of a man's ministry.

Yet, the creative person will often find a challenge in the most unchallenging situation. The ministry of the renowned German pastor Wilhelm Loehe is an example in point. Because he was too independent as a young man, he was sent by his theological superiors to a crude peasant community as a form of exile. But Loehe found enough challenge there to remain for his entire ministry. He created out of what was considered next to nothing—Neuendettelsau—a religious community that was to become known throughout the world for its missionary contributions to the Church.

Whenever there is a creative person or a creative situation, there will always be a problem about time. Creation by its definition is unlimited, and time is by definition a limitation. Creation is always increasing, evolving, while time is always decreasing, closing in. The creative aspect of the ministry is continually in tension with time's inflexible boundaries of death and deadlines. While there may be some weeks when the minister can adapt his work to be able to march from Selma to Montgomery, there are others when the unscheduled interruption of sickness and death turns the creative nature of his ministry into a siege of compassionate comfort for the dying and sustenance for the bereaved, so that even the deadline of Sunday morning is temporarily blocked out by the intense interpersonal involvement.

"Father" Is a Relevant Title

The ministry is like parenthood. As any frustrated parent knows, his children feel they never get enough of him. Says Christopher Robin in *Now We Are Six:*

> Well, I'm very fond of Daddy, but he hasn't time to play.
> And I'm very fond of Mummy, but she sometimes goes away.[2]

Each child feels deprived and resents it. Nor is there any way to avoid the situation. The desire is insatiable and sharing is abhorred. Older children—the terrible teen-agers—may seem to reverse things. They feel they have too much parent. Actually these older children simply require more skill from the parent in giving to them. As every youth counselor knows, the adolescent is very miffed at his parents for any withholding of their time and interest.

The title Father for the clergyman is anything but irrelevant. His parental problem is complicated, however, by the size of his family. But like the youngsters in his own home, he finds them starved for his attention and appreciation, and quick to notice any slight or any preference. "We never see him," they say. "He hasn't been around for ages. I guess he doesn't have time for *some* of us. He's just interested in the new people." His problem is further complicated by his own need to please—to be liked—and being dependent upon signs that he is succeeding in this regard. This dependency is a handicap to effective parenthood. The parent who needs assurance that his children believe he is a good parent is too dependent to exercise his parental responsibility. Such dependency is likewise an obstacle to an effective ministry.

If you are a faithful layman in your congregation, you know what it means to be taken for granted by the minister. It has probably been obvious to you that the less faithful member gets more attention. He receives something akin to honorable mention whenever he gets around to fulfilling an obligation which you fulfill on a regular basis. You have biblical precedent for your concern. In the parable of the prodigal son, the elder brother fulfilled his obligations to his father by working steadily on the farm and not "bugging" him for his inheritance. The younger brother shirked his duties, persuaded his father to give him his share of the inheritance, and then proceeded to waste it in riotous living. But who received the ring, the best robe, the fatted calf, and the party? And why? Simply because, after he had "gone broke," he returned to take up the duties his older brother had been doing all the time. No wonder the brother asked, "I've been here all the time working away, but who gets the fatted calf? I never even got a kid! You have never given me a party! Why should I rejoice at *his* party?" So it shall always be. There is more joy in heaven over one sinner who repents than over ninety and nine just persons who need no repentance.

The Faithful Members Are Brushed Off

So when the minister brushes by you with a brief nod in order to pump the hand of the inactive member who finally managed to show up, or the new member, or even the visitor, remember that it is "par for the course." It takes a good deal of maturity to endure the neglect that comes from being a consistent church worker, who does not at the moment have a key position in the congregational leadership. One might even gather the impression that consistent means colorless.

Actually the minister is overrating you. He assumes that, because you are a faithful church member, you have no particular needs. If you have such needs, you will have to take the initiative to bring them to his attention. This, of course, raises the problem of disturbing his positive image of you. I receive letters from people who begin by saying, "Our pastor thinks we are a very happy family, and I don't want to disturb this impression. Therefore, I am writing to you instead." However, if his image of you is altered because of what you tell him, you will at least get more attention. So when you are neglected by your minister, it is really the greatest compliment he could pay you. It means he thinks you are "in the groove."

Demands Can Be Tortuous

The unending demands that are in the very nature of the minister's work easily cause him to become anxious over getting it all done, and to feel guilty over the unfinished business. The result is frustration over the many pressures demanding attention. This poses the need for him to learn to live with incompletion—if he is going to live at all. In the ministry the dominant seventh chord may hang in the air for a long time before it is resolved, and the second shoe may not drop on the floor above when we think it should to complete the story of the first drop. The minister may have to go to sleep in this state of suspension. Obviously such a life is not the ideal situation for a perfectionist.

Besides being unending, the demands can be tortuous. There are matters that need his attention, but how to go about them? The family whom the pastor knows is having domestic troubles—should he go to them? Would it not be better if they came to him? Those who inform him about the problem usually do so in a "you should do something about it" way. He feels the coercion, and wishes the informer would take more responsibility. But informing the pastor seems to be all he plans to do. He wishes those who had the problem would take the initiative and contact him. But they don't!

In the meantime he waits—and worries. Which way is the passing of time taking him—to or from a solution? Is he losing valuable time in "stewing" about it—or will "stewing" lead to "brewing" a better idea? He realizes all too well that he can act too hastily in these matters and feels the tension between the scriptural directives "Wait on the Lord" and "Now is the accepted time." As much as he tries to keep his own problems out of it, he cannot help but wonder how he will be judged—by people, by God, by himself—if something should happen before he makes his move—divorce action, scandal, violence, suicide? Is he then being moved by wisdom or pressure, by love or guilt, by courage or fear, by compassion or self-defense?

Idolatrous Tendencies

The struggle for time is further intensified by the pastor's idolatrous tendencies. I John's closing admonition, "Little children, keep yourselves from idols," is easier said than done. Like Martha of Bethany, the pastor is cumbered about with so many things that he loses sight of the one thing needful. In his sermons he usually applies this story of Mary and Martha to women who become overinvolved in the cares of homemaking. Yet, like most men, he can become quite upset if his supper is late—or burned! The tendency to become "cumbered about with much serving" is no respecter of the sexes. It can grow out of self-idolatry, that is, out of the need to establish our self-worth by our busyness. The fact that we become anxious and troubled about these many things adds to our sense of self-importance. Also the very bind into which our busyness places us provides a sop to our conscience over our procrastination in imposing specific changes into our way of living. Most of us plan to do things better as soon as we are not so busy. Therefore, the very busyness that we protest we also perpetuate in a defensive need to maintain the *status quo.*

It is easy for the minister to become lost in his parish world and not be able to see beyond it. His parish-centricity becomes an extension of his egocentricity. The anxiety he experiences over the many problems of his parish world is the evidence that none of these is the one thing needful. It has been suggested that the minister is more likely to have come from a clerical or working-class family than a professional or executive family, and therefore is constantly resisting his busyness on the basis of the eight-hour workday.[3] In other words he fights the professional man's work schedule because he unconsciously identifies with the work hours of the run-of-the-mill employee. There is probably some truth to his contention, although the percentage of ministers who come from the parsonage itself is high, though not as high as it once was. Also the number who come from the farm or the small shopkeeping class is significant, particularly in the Midwest—and there is no eight-hour workday in either of these occupations.

Recently I heard the problem expressed from a different perspective. A group of seminary administrators were noting that their students were coming more and more from the middle and even the upper-middle class. "You should see the number of parents who arrive in Cadillacs for commencement," said one. How then, they ask, can these men minister to the poor when they do not know what it means to be poor? The previous generation could at least remember the Depression.

Regardless of what may or may not be the influence from his background, the fact remains that the minister's work schedule poses a real problem. He may long for the time when there is *no* schedule, no press. Our seminary conducts a chautauqua-like conference for pastors each summer. Noticing a minister at this occasion wandering around aimlessly, I asked him if he would like to become involved in one of the activities planned for that hour. "No," he said with a serene smile, "I'm just enjoying *being*—and being without a telephone."

But a little of this goes a long way. It usually is not long before the agony of nothing being accomplished—of wasting time—of getting behind—begins. So back he goes to his schedule and organization. But after weeks of this he may begin to agonize again—this time over the loss of spontaneity and enjoyment in his life. "Is this living?" he asks his wife. It is not likely that she will give him much argument.

The Light Touch of a Child

Anxiety is characterized by our awareness that time is "crowding in." The words "too late," "past the deadline," "getting behind schedule," and "missing out" are fear words —symbols of nonbeing. Time becomes primarily a matter of its quantitative dimension. On the other hand, enjoyment is largely unconscious of this dimension of time. Its positive involvement is an experience of time's qualitative dimension. The anxious person is preoccupied with the quantitative aspect of time because he feels the pressure to prove himself. His self-worth—his success—depends upon his accomplishment. Since time is the medium within which his accomplishment must take place, he may lose the appreciation for the qualitative dimension of time when under pressure to "get things done." With his self-worth at stake, he takes himself too seriously and develops a "heavy touch" in his work.

In contrast, when a person experiences enjoyment, he loses this tension. Like a child, he then is conscious of time primarily in its qualitative dimension. The concept of "hurry" is foreign to a child until he finally succumbs to the prodding of the adult world. Yet, Jesus pointed to a child as the expression of human greatness. "Whoever does not receive

the Kingdom of God like a child," He said, "shall not enter
it." (Mark 10:15) The "light touch" of the child is an expression of his childlike faith. His enjoyment of his Father's
world is inseparable from his security in his Father's world.
Childhood, therefore, is not only something we go from—but
something we go toward. Enjoyment is probably closer to
whatever we mean by human perfection than accomplishment, and anxiety over accomplishment may be the most
telltale symptom of idolatry.

Positive and Negative Involvement

In spite of the values of childhood, the fact remains that
the minister, like the rest of us, is under adult rather than
childhood obligations. Accomplishment is simply not an op-
tion for him. Can accomplishment and enjoyment be com-
bined on the adult level? Can the qualitative and the
quantitative aspects of time be united in the adult consciousness without the one canceling out the other?

The answer is *yes* if one has a creative approach to his
work. Then his work will be more than the doing of an
activist. It will involve also the qualitative concern of the
artist. Though exhausting, it is not anxiety-producing. The
exhaustion is an integrated exhaustion due to spending oneself rather than a disintegrated exhaustion due to fighting
oneself. An example of such spending of oneself is the exhaustion that a pastor experiences in his pastoral care. Pulled
out of himself by his identification with the needs of another, he may exhaust his emotional energies in his concern
with the crisis. Yet, his is also the satisfaction of meaningful
—qualitative—experience.

The opposite of involvement is the boredom and indifference of the uninvolved and the uncommitted, who believe
that time requires artificial stimulation to offset its intermi-
nable drag. The opposite of *positive* involvement is the negative involvement of anxiety that downgrades trust in God

and man. When we take ourselves too seriously we develop anxiety over our concerns. Ours is a spiritualized egocentricity which upgrades our sense of indispensability. "In cares and pleasures," says the hymn, "Christian love me more than these." Adapted to the clergy it could read, "In the cares and pleasures of the congregation, Pastor love me more than these." The kingdom of God is in these cares and pleasures, but it also extends beyond them, and if we confine it to them, we lose the kingdom and create an idol.

Busy or Disorganized

"How are you? Busy, I suppose," said a minister in greeting a fellow minister. "No," replied the other, "not busy, just disorganized." Our busyness may be due to our disorganization as much as anything. One can be organized and creative even as he can be anxiety-ridden and disorganized. Organization may be the mark of integration. It may also be an indication of compulsive tendencies. Because the Christian is *in* the world does not mean that he has to be *of* it. Nor does the fact that he is not *of* the world mean that he is not *in* it. If the minister is an executive—and in the current parish structure, he is—then he ought to follow executive procedures. He can develop an efficient ministry without making efficiency the object of his ministry.

Efficiency in itself simply means concentration in one's efforts. For example, efficiency in pastoral work means concentrating this ministry for those who are consciously in need. It is in our crises that our sense of self-sufficiency is low and we are open, and often desirous, for the support of the ministry. On the other hand, when things are going well our defenses are usually well intact.

Much of the pressure of the ministry is due more to the lack of discipline in concentration than to much work. Because he was so upset over the press of his work, a certain minister felt he had to see a psychiatrist or have a nervous breakdown. The psychiatrist asked him to list all the things that he had to do that he did not seem able to get done. Taking the first item on the list—to obtain a choir director— he said, "I want you to leave now and do just one thing. Get a choir director. Then come back." In this manner he took him down the list and when he was through the minister was well. All the psychiatrist did was organize him.

When things pile up we tend to worry about all of them instead of concentrating on one of them. When our concentration is divided, our efficiency is poor. We have great ideas, but little carry-through. We are prone to start things but not to complete them. The answer to the worship of efficiency is not inefficiency, but the worship of God. Faith helps us carry through when for lack of encouragement we would quit. Commitment helps us to become involved through the concentration of self-giving in the concerns of the ministry. But faith is not necessarily separated from wisdom. Our good intentions, even motivations, need a plan of procedure.

Following the practice of the psychiatrist, the pastor may plan an activity schedule at the beginning of each day. In this way he is relieved of the pressure that something is being overlooked and can concentrate on the task at hand. It is wise to make a carbon of the list in case he misplaces it during the day. The schedule is a guide for the pastor's concentration, and not a list of activities he feels compelled to carry out. Like any plan for action, it needs to be used with a degree of flexibility. The schedule is made for the minister and not the minister for the schedule.

Flexibility

A flexible person uses a schedule flexibly, not compulsively. Compulsive people are more like machines than persons, driven by guilt rather than by electricity or gasoline. If the machine ever becomes the master of man, it will be because man himself has become a machine. It is one thing to be a determined person and another to be a driven person. The one is an expression of human freedom and the other an expression of human bondage. The schedule is for the day at hand. Things may happen in this day that were not foreseen by the schedule-maker. While each moment is influenced by the past, it brings enough uniqueness into being to require a present, on the spot, evaluation. In contrast to a rigid person who finds great difficulty in adjusting to any change in plans, the flexible person is free to evaluate the present moment on its own merits and not simply on his preconception of that moment.

The inability to follow an activity schedule, like the inability to deviate from it, is indicative of inner resistance to do anything more than lament over our difficulties. These two extremes stand out in bold relief in the ministry of calling. The pastor who is driven by his mission board or by his inner compulsion to prove he is a "go-getter," tends to measure his visits by the clock because he is counting the number of his calls. He bypasses quality for quantity, believing that doing is the equivalent of doing well. By piling up the quantitatives, he believes that quality is sure to follow. In the back of his mind he is thinking about the statistical forms he must fill out at the end of the year for his denominational report. It is hoped his record will show "progress."

The opposite extreme is the pastor who seems unable to make a break in the conversation to bring his visit to a close. He is the "door-knob holder," whose second round begins once he reaches the door. Were his prolonged visit a matter of losing himself in the relationship, it would be different. More than likely it is simply his inability to assert himself. He feels that, when he takes the initiative to leave, even though he is the caller, he is showing a disregard for the people, or at least that they may interpret it in this way. People help foster this impression by saying such nonsensical things as "Must you go so soon?" or "Don't feel you have to hurry!" whenever he makes a move in the direction of the door. Of course they do not want him to take them seriously. They feel if they do not show reluctance at his gesture to leave, they may offend him. But the poor fellow does take them seriously, and when he does, they pay for their duplicity.

The pastor should question whether his reluctance to offend is not an overcompensation. People who seek to reduce all the threats to others in their approach to them may be trying to cover their tracks. The irony of the illusion is that the minister who stays longer than he intended because he does not want to give the impression that he has no time for these people does not realize that they wish he would leave. The fear of displeasing leads to displeasing. The need to please hinders our perception of the dynamics of the moment. We read into them rather than read them. This compulsion to guard against anything that may be threatening to others is an obstacle to love.

Some of us need to be in a bind—to feel under pressure —to produce. The tendency was prevalent in seminary when we found it next to impossible to get down to work on term papers until the deadline was dangerously close. Then we discovered we could release ourselves for an all-out effort, vowing at the same time never to let it happen again. But we could not seem to keep that vow! We simply had no efficiency when we attempted to work ahead of schedule or even on schedule. Why? Seemingly we have the need for an external conflict against which to integrate our energies. Obviously one cannot integrate himself against an inner conflict. So we sabotage our time until we can project the conflict to the outside. The dread of *something*, the external conflict, be it a deadline, a meeting, a sick call, is always better than the dread of *nothing*, the inner conflict.

It is to our advantage to challenge this cycle of sabotage. Not only does our confrontation with the dread of nothing hold the key to victory in the struggle for time, it also brings us face to face with the source of the conflict from which Christ came to redeem us. When this conflict over ourselves is brought to the light of divine grace, we are one step nearer to the peace that passes understanding. Then we are no longer running, even from our own judgment, and are in a position to preserve the balance between mechanization and spontaneity, between continuity and vitality, between efficiency and ecstasy.

X. LIVING THE BALANCED LIFE

Whenever a minister attempts to put into words his negative feelings toward the parish ministry, his usual lament is that he is burdened with a lot of inconsequential activity. The implication is that he is powerless to do anything about it. Pessimism rather than optimism is the dominant sentiment of our day. It provides a solace for our anxieties while optimism stirs them up. None of us likes to be told that he is more free—and therefore more responsible—than he would like to think, but the fact is that the minister *can* do something about this situation.

In the first place, whether an activity is inconsequential or not is determined as much by our attitude toward it as by the activity itself. Often we fail to see the religious significance of our experience because we have too narrow a view of the religious. Instead we look with scorn on the social encounters that fill our day as though they were purely mundane, and therefore beside the point. Perhaps they are—but this may be due to our having prejudged them rather than being open to their potential.

In the second place, even if the activities are inconsequential, the minister can do more than he thinks to change things. In the final analysis he has as much influence as the congregation and even as church headquarters in shaping his own ministry. But he may have to act with a good deal of firmness and courage to make his influence determinative.

Busyness as a Cover

There is the need on occasion for the pastor to strip his schedule to the essentials. The never-ending pileup of things to be done is abetted by the psychology of busyness. Being busy with a myriad of tasks provides us with the security which we seek. It is our most popular antidote to anxiety. Besides being the badge of importance, busyness is also the best defense against doing the things we know we should if we had the time. The prospect of having the time is really quite frightening. Every pastor owes it to his own growth to have this experience.

Busyness provides us with a ready-made structure for our day-by-day living. Most of us have a fear of the unstructured moment. It leaves the door open to the unpredictable and the unexpected—confronting us with decisions that we are not pressured by circumstances to make. Busyness makes our decisions for us. "What choice do I have?" we say. "It's not that I don't want to, it's that I can't!" But what if we could? Would we then want to? Busyness protects us from even raising this question. "It's not my fault, I'm helpless." When there is no alternative to a decision, it is not really a decision. Or rather it is the decision to accept the inevitable. This releases us from responsibility and therefore from guilt. As long as the busyness continues we remain secure, and the pressure upon us to change is kept to a minimum.

The never-ending pileup is also encouraged by our tendency to believe in our own indispensability. It may help to ask ourselves what would happen if we became ill for a week. It is rather deflating to realize that things would go on, regardless. In fact the lay leadership in some congregations has come to life because of the necessity created by the pastor's absence. The lay leader could ask himself the same question. While I was its pastor, a congregation decided to pioneer a mission at the growing edge of the community. When the list of volunteers to establish the mission was complete, it included three fourths of our church council and two thirds of our Sunday school staff. Several in the congregation were on the verge of panic. Would we have anything left? Within one week all of the vacancies were filled. People who never had the opportunity before responded to the invitation to serve. New talent was discovered. We not only survived, but within one year we had regained our financial support and our numbers in membership. So the church and the community will survive if we cut down to a bare minimum for a season.

In the rat race in which most of us find ourselves, we tend to lose our sense of values. Newscaster Paul Harvey, in announcing the death of seventy-seven people in a plane crash, said, "Seventy-seven people dead—and all alive yesterday, and probably worrying about the wrong things." In his first letter to the Corinthians, St. Paul has some frightening things to say to any church worker. "No other foundation can anyone lay than that which is laid, which is Jesus Christ. Now if anyone builds on the foundation with gold, silver, precious stones, wood, hay, stubble—each man's work will become manifest; for the Day will disclose it, because it will be revealed with fire, and the fire will test what sort of work each one has done." (I Cor. 3:11–13)

In our work are we building with stone or stubble? It clarifies the situation just to ask the question. Yet it is frightening because it questions what we like to assume without questioning. "I've been getting around a lot of church dedications in recent years," said a prominent churchman, "and invariably thanks are offered because God has 'blessed' them with a new building. But how do we know it's a blessing— from God?" Even to raise this question might be enough to undercut the building fund!

We tend to "sanctify" our rut in order to stay in it. Having the need to justify our anxiety, we call it conscientiousness. We need to do something about our compulsion to feel important and so we speak about our high calling to the holy ministry. To live with our failure to keep up with our modern scholarship, we say with vehemence, "God's Word never changes!" What we mean is, "How dare anyone infer that something has happened in theological education since I was in seminary!" To sanctify our hidden martyr complex we lament over our unending obligations.

Blowing Too Many Horns

In explaining his desire to leave the parish ministry for a specialized ministry, a pastor said, "I have a great pastoral challenge in my congregation, but I have no time to work it. There is so much in the parish ministry that is really not the ministry. I can't do the work that I have been educated to do." His complaint corresponds to the findings of a study of 690 pastors by Samuel Blizzard. These ministers worked on the average of ten hours a day, four of which were spent in administration, compared to thirty-six minutes on sermon preparation. Yet the work that was least enjoyed by these men was the role of organizer and administrator. The work they had been educated to do—preacher, pastor, priest—received the least amount of time.[1]

Joseph Sittler speaks about the "maceration of the minister." His work is so chopped up into small pieces that he can "blow any horn one hands him."[2] In my own denomination he was handed a real horn. Church headquarters sent out a plastic ram's horn of jubilee which he was to blow before the congregation to celebrate the first anniversary of the synodical merger and to inaugurate a year of ingathering for special funds. Like the classic definition of hell, the minister's function under the chopper can become simply "one damn thing after another."

The minister has an ambivalence over the functions of organization and administration. Although he complains about the large amount of time these functions require, he continues to hold on to them. In administration and organization there is power and one is reluctant to give it up. To delegate this work means to move over, and subconsciously we tend to resist this. The authority in the tangible world of administration is easier to accept than the authority in the intangible world of faith. Instead of adding another clergy-man to its staff, growing congregations would be wiser in my opinion if they followed the example of some few churches who have hired instead a lay executive secretary or business manager, so that the minister can concentrate on his ministry.

Strip Down to Essentials by Delegating

In order to strip to the essentials, the minister will have to delegate—or drop—everything except those responsibil-ities uniquely associated with his office. Besides being a help to the minister, this strip-down may also become an oppor-tunity for others. We assume some of our obligations be-cause it is less trouble than working with someone else. Some of us hate to ask another to do anything. We will put notices in the church bulletin, drop innuendos from the pul-pit, or try to get others to do the asking. Yet, the personal request of the minister is the most effective way. Being the VIP of the congregation, he in a sense is honoring the mem-ber whom he asks for help. This does not necessarily mean that the person will accede to the request—although most of the time he will. But it does mean that the minister and the church program are not the only ones that are receiving in the transaction.

The efficiency of the administration of President Lyndon Johnson centers in the personal contact that Johnson culti-vates with those with whom he must work. The efficiency of James A. Farley as a political organizer was related to his ability to call people by name. These personal approaches can be used as gimmicks to manipulate people into a smooth-working machine, either political or ecclesiastical. They can also, however, be manifestations of a fellowship where the personal is the essential tie. The attraction of the early Church was its *koinonia*, or fellowship. Here was its grass roots, unstructured, evangelism program. It is not the

mimeographed invitation or the "personal" letter run off by
the automatic typewriter that conveys *koinonia*, but the personal contact, the name, the individual, the honest concern.
Love is not directed to people, but to persons. The pastor's
example in this regard is contagious within the congregation
as the members begin to reflect his spirit.

The involvement of others in the program of the church is
beneficial to *them*—providing they are not the "same few."
While these few usually are capable people, they are sometimes slow to surrender their tasks or even to share them.
They may complain quite rightly that they are bearing too
much of the load because others are not accepting their
share, but they may also have their doubts whether these
others can do as well. Giving these others the opportunity
may prove that they can. It is beneficial also to the faithful
few if they share the load, for it helps them to experience
the cooperative membership of the Body. Sometimes the
few prefer to do things by themselves rather than to work
with others. They do it well—but the projects then tend to
become their own personal contributions, if not possessions.
The important thing in the Church is that we work together
as members one of another. For as Paul says, "The eye
cannot say to the hand, 'I have no need of you,' nor again
the head to the feet, 'I have no need of you.'" The body
in which all of the functioning is concentrated in a few members is a sick body, as the active members become distorted
and enlarged and the inactive atrophy. Therefore God has
adjusted the body, says Paul, to balance honor and function,
"that there may be no discord in the body, but that the members may have the same care for one another." (I Cor. 12:
21–26)

In order to strip to the essentials the minister will have
to overcome his guilt over not being present at every gathering. As long as he is uneasy over his absence, as though he
was shirking his duty, he probably will not feel right unless
he attends. But for his own development he should examine

this guilt. What is he trying to prove by his omnipresence? Some ministers frankly admit that they are afraid of what may happen if they are not present. "You never know what these laymen are going to do when they are on their own," said one. "I actually save time by being present. It's the ounce of prevention that is worth the pound of cure." I think every minister would understand his concern. Yet, if the congregation is being held together by the minister's omnipresence, how long can it hold? And how can its lay leadership develop when it is not trusted?

Others acknowledge that their guilt over not being present is the old fear of being criticized for goldbricking. Their presence, therefore, is in defense of the ministerial image. Kierkegaard said that the Judas No. 2 of Christendom is he who first invented the notion of defending Christianity. He who defends it, says Kierkegaard, has never believed it. So he who feels compelled to defend his Christian ministry— or even worse, somebody else's image of the Christian ministry—has no clear conviction of his own. Therefore, he is trying to adjust his role—defend it—to those who seem to know. Is it any wonder then that he feels curtailed by the parish ministry? When he has at least as clear an idea of his role as he believes his congregation has, he will have a basis for freeing himself to affirm himself.

Restore the Soul to the Body

After the minister has stripped his activities to the essentials, he is in a position to live a balanced life. Having put his schedule through the threshing machine, he has gotten rid of the stubble and can get to the grain. There is a need for balance in our activities if we are to preserve our spiritual and emotional health. In the wisdom of Ecclesiastes there is a time for work, a time for family, a time for recreation socially and physically, and a time for worship and meditation. Life is life in the body, even for the minister. I

had a dentist friend who lectured me at each visit to his office on the necessity for caring for one's physical health.
"Ministers," he complained, "are notorious for neglecting
their 'physical self,' while stressing the importance of the
'spiritual self.'" In his way of thinking this was the equivalent of blasphemy.

Although he had no statistics to back up his charge and
depended instead upon his own experience with ministers,
the dentist probably had a point. The neglect of the body
is an old "Christian" sin. It stems from the ancient dichot-
omy of body and soul that the early Church assimilated
from the Asian and Grecian cultures. Because the body was
considered to be the prison house of the soul, the religions of
the world had worked for centuries to release the soul from
the influence of the body. Now that we are realizing once
again the biblical conception of man as a total person, we
are attempting to restore the soul to the body. If man is a
total person, then not only is there no separation between
his body and his soul, there is also no separation between his
religious and secular life. If man is one in all of his parts,
then his life is religious in all of its activities. To neglect any
phase of life is irreligious, for religion is the integrator of all
of life.

For our day of imbalance there is scarcely a better way
for the pastor to lead a good example than in living a balanced life. Some people notice the way he lives more than
they listen to what he says. His example of balance is particularly valuable for the men in his parish. They may tend
to think that ministers are of a different breed of men who
live on an other-worldly plane inhabited mostly by asexual
women and anemic although saintly men. As the regular
breed of men neglect their family responsibilities and the
nurture of their souls to establish themselves in the life of
the world, so the minister neglects his family responsibilities
and his physical self for the life of the Spirit. The pastor's
example in balanced living is a counteractive to this un-

happy division. It is an example in being human—something from which both the other-worldly saint and the man of the world fall short. The pastor's family would also benefit from his balanced life, and this in turn benefits the pastor. When their needs are being satisfied, they respond by satisfying his needs.

His example in living the balanced life will also attract more young men to the ministry. For several years many of us have watched with alarm the declining numbers in our theological seminaries. I have attended many meetings called for the purpose of looking into this problem. We ask each other why there is a decline and what can be done about it. The conclusions reached usually center around the awareness that the image of the minister in our society is low. Therefore the men who are ministers must be contributing to this image and consequently hold the key to its change. As I talk with young men about considering the ministry they express concern about this image. They see the minister as living an unnatural life. He is set apart—not from sin—but from the common life, and they feel "shut out" from this image. Actually they feel too normal for what seems to be an abnormal albeit holy existence. God became one of us in Jesus Christ to sanctify the common and not to remove us from it. The balanced life is the lived-out experience of the full life that God has given us and has redeemed for us in Christ.

The Inertia of Habit

In the ministry an imbalance often occurs. Sickness and death are not scheduled, nor are domestic problems. Funerals, weddings, hospital calls, and family crises can pile up and completely absorb a week or weeks. The idea, however, is to return to a balance as soon as possible. The danger lies in the inertia of habit. Once we are unbalanced, our very imbalance takes on the appearance of normality. It becomes the norm around which the conscience begins to operate. The minister has a sense of guilt unless he is *doing* —at the momentum to which he has become accustomed. As one pastor confessed, "I've gotten so that I can't take any time off. All the time I feel uneasy—actually guilty—like I should be *doing* something." The very experience of momentary inaction automatically makes him uneasy. This is a vivid demonstration of what it means dynamically to believe that one is justified only by his works.

Ours is an age of the anxiety of emptiness and meaninglessness. Being a part of his age, the minister partakes of its disease. Busyness provides the illusion of meaningfulness. An unscheduled pause in the busyness may bring up the specter of meaningless again. Hence the almost desperate need to keep going. The need for a cause may grow out of this same anxiety. The cause—whether it be civil rights, fighting communism, the proposed educational unit, or liturgical reforms—provides the meaning for our life that preserves us from despondency. If we need the cause to integrate ourselves against our own anxiety, we can hardly be giving ourselves to the cause. Rather the cause is giving itself to us. The real need is the need to *be*—and to enjoy *being*. But to meet this need requires more than a temporary cause to which to devote our energies. It is not those who are looking for a cause that, finding it, serve it well, but those who find it forced upon them because of their convictions.

Psychiatrist Viktor Frankl has developed his logotherapy on the conviction that our life has to have meaning. He quotes Nietzsche to the effect that "he who has a *why* to live can bear with almost any *how*."[3] Frankl's own *why* enabled him to endure the terrible *how* of the Nazi concentration camp. The *why* has to come from deeper sources than a temporary cause. Frankl's term logotherapy comes from the word *logos* (word) which has an ancient philosophical history. The *Word* is the integrating meaning of

life that gives my life its meaning. St. John saw its impli-
cations for the Christian Gospel. "In the beginning was the
Word, and the Word was with God, and the Word was God
. . . And the Word became flesh and dwelt among us, full
of grace and truth." (John 1:1, 14) God redeemed our common life by joining himself to it so that its meaning might
extend beyond it. He took upon himself human flesh to rec-
oncile us to our own being. Our meaning is inseparable from
this reconciliation.

Since this meaning is from within, it gives meaning to that
which is without. We see what we see in terms of this meaning rather than trying to find meaning in what we see. "For
with thee is the fountain of life," says the psalmist, and "in
thy light do we see light." (Ps. 36:9) Through this experience of meaning we can see the religious significance in
what might otherwise be considered insignificant.

Only by persisting in taking time off for other activities
can the pastor who feels guilty when not working finally
overcome the inertia of his habit pattern. He must not allow the demands of the ministry to drown out his awareness
that he is not really exerting an all-out effort to achieve the
full life. His whole emphasis has been on *becoming*—on
progress—rather than on *being*. Yet the irony is that there
can be no genuine becoming until one is reconciled with
being. This is simply another way of saying that he can perform no works that are pleasing to God until he is justified
by grace. Until one can *be,* his *doing* (becoming) is an escape rather than an outgrowth from *being*. Prior to the
call to the ministry—and undergirding it—is the call to *be*.

The Tyranny of Conscience

In striving for the balanced life the minister as well as
the layman needs to learn to recognize Satan. The saying
of Jesus, "Get behind me, Satan," is the most powerful of
exorcisms. God and the devil get mixed up in our mental

image of the deity. Our conscience is responsible for this confusion. To the degree that we are unreconciled with our being, God is pictured as an enemy. The tyrannical conscience is the unreconciled conscience that is compulsively set to placate the hostile deity. Before the conscience can function on the basis of love, it is necessary that it be reconciled with God on the basis of His love. Then the image of God as love is formed. As Christians we affirm our reconciliation with God, but most of us still struggle inwardly with unreconciled guilt. Learning to recognize Satan is learning to recognize these demands of unreconciled conscience as "of the devil."

As usual, Satan is disguised as an angel of light—this time as the compulsion to be a success. There is anxiety behind this drive because we are in a race against death. Without success there is only nothingness. In the search for reconciliation through achievement, there is pressure to succeed before it is too late. But achievement promises more than it gives. The quest is doomed from the start because the value of an achievement is only temporary. Soon the pressure begins again for another, and bigger, achievement. Here is where we need to defy the pressure in the name of Christ. Recognizing it for what it is, we can say with Christ, "Get behind me, Satan!"—yes, even throw the ink bottle at him as Luther did. For this pressure comes from a conscience that Paul says is "under the law," and therefore is a distorted conscience.

Nietzsche also recognized the tyranny of the conscience under the law and saw that only by defying it could we become free. Otherwise we grovel in the dust as lowly debtors to the God of the bad conscience. The way to freedom is to get rid of God. Nietzsche looks forward to the "complete and eventual triumph of atheism freeing mankind from all this feeling of obligation to their origin."[4] We can improve on Nietzsche's solution even if we have to agree with his diagnosis of what he called "the disease called man." The grace of Christ, which Nietzsche thought only enslaved man in a more subtle way, actually frees him. It frees him to defy not God but God's distorted image, the devil. The purpose in such defiance is not the will to power as Nietzsche thought, but the will to love.

The balanced life has a way of reducing tension. Our tensions are often protests against unsatisfied needs. The protests become disguised as tensions when they are not listened to directly. The fact that, though unheeded, they return in disguise is indicative that they shall be heard, though not necessarily recognized. Despite the lesser amount of time the pastor allots to his task, he is more able to cope with it. When he is involved, he is more involved because there is less protest—resistance—from the imbalance. The amount of time we put in is not the decisive factor if our efficiency is diminished by the increase of internal friction and its subsequent wear and tear on the body.

When our human needs are being met through a balanced living, the tasks of the parish are not so likely to get mixed up with our own needs. Layman and minister alike are predisposed to use their church work to prove their worth, to themselves, other people, and God, when their conscience is yet under the law. They have need for a cause to champion in order to give importance to themselves because as naked beings they feel unacceptable and impoverished. Because his own needs are being met, the clergyman as well as the layman is more effective in his ministry to others. The more his own needs as a human being are satisfied, the more *agape* love he is able to live.

"God Is Not Dead!"

The minister is a minister of the Word of God. What then does this Word of God say to the minister? It says that in the midst of parish problems God *is*—that He is *here*—acting in the present moment whether or not I can recognize His movement or understand His way. When Luther became discouraged at one point in his reformational activities, his wife, Katie, is supposed to have said to him, "Martin, God is not dead!" The mighty acts of God which we as a Church proclaim are not confined to the past—to some uniquely religious period in history called sacred history. God is the Lord of all history and is acting now in the making of history. The present moment has always been the hardest time in which to recognize God's action. The psalmist experienced the desolation of this moment when he lamented, "Will the Lord spurn forever and never again be favorable? Has his steadfast love forever ceased? Are his promises at an end for all time? Has God forgotten to be gracious? Has he in anger shut up his compassion?" In this barren moment he turns his mind to the past—when God had acted. "I will call to mind the deeds of the Lord; yea, I will remember thy wonders of old." (Ps. 77:7-9, 11) So it is by faith rather than by sight that we believe in the sovereignty of God in the present event.

But this faith has little support in our modern secular world. In fact even theologians are beginning to waver. A current theological movement on the American scene says that for all meaningful purposes God is dead—as dead as Nietzsche said He was. Even the word God is unreal for our age. He is absent from our current experience and therefore it is irrelevant even to talk about Him. We can talk about Jesus since He was seen and heard in our tangible midst—but not about God. In other words we should confine our religious beliefs to what is verifiable in our secular culture.

While we may draw back from such a bold assertion from within the Church that God is dead, these theologians may have a point. As far as being a factor in modern secular thinking, God may as well be dead. As one of our noted preachers put it, "The Church really cuts very little ice where the decisions that count in our world are made: In the board rooms of banks and corporations, in legislatures and city councils, in the high councils of labor unions. And even in the daily decisions made by ordinary people every day, in hiring and firing, buying and selling, taking a job or turning it down, in voting booths or in those private chambers of the safety deposit vaults at the local bank, how often, do you think, does Christian commitment seriously affect these daily decisions?"[5] These words are a reflection upon the layman, for it is he who is in the board rooms of banks, in city councils, and in the councils of labor unions. This sorry state of affairs confirms the contemporary assumption that the Church is confined to what goes on in the church building. The next logical assumption is that God is also confined there. And if He is, He is dead—at least He is no longer the sovereign Lord of heaven and earth.

It is not God who is dead. It is we who have died to Him. God is—whether we believe He is or not. Yet He is alive *for us* when we live in the awareness of His presence and sovereignty. This means that the Church is *in* the board rooms of banks, in city councils, in the councils of labor unions, as much if not more than it is in the building with the cross on it. It is at the office, in the factory, and in the social halls. The minister's task is not primarily to run the program in the building, it is to equip the lay ministry, the lay witness for the exercising of its Christian commitment in the hiring and firing, buying and selling in our secularized society. When this is our understanding of the Church and its ministry, we will not only ask what the minister we have hired is doing with his time, we will ask also what we are doing with *ours*.

The Word of God has something to say to our ministerial crisis, for it has something to say to the harassed minister. It is part of his pastoral care of himself to allow this Word to say it. The Word is communicated in words—hence, our Bible. I would suggest the following verses as typical for the purpose of acknowledging the reality of the living God.

1. "I am the Lord thy God . . . Thou shalt have no other gods before me." (Exodus 5:6–7)

2. "First cast out the beam out of thine own eye; and then shalt thou see clearly to cast out the mote out of thy brother's eye." (Matt. 7:5)

3. "Love one another as I have loved you." (John 15:12)

4. "Fret not yourself; it tends only to evil." (Ps. 37:8)

5. "Have no anxiety about anything, but in everything by prayer and supplication with thanksgiving let your requests be made known to God." (Phil. 4:6)

6. "Let the peace of God rule in your hearts . . . and be ye thankful." (Col. 3:15)

7. "Trust in the Lord with all thine heart; and lean not unto thine own understanding. In all thy ways acknowledge him, and he shall direct thy paths." (Prov. 3:5–6)

8. "I can do all things through Christ which strengtheneth me." (Phil. 4:13)

NOTES

CHAPTER ONE

1. Copyright 1957 Christian Century Foundation. Reprinted by permission from the April 24, 1957, issue of *The Christian Century*, p. 531.
2. Copyright 1957 Christian Century Foundation. Reprinted by permission from the May 22, 1957, issue of *The Christian Century*, p. 659.
3. *The Lutheran Standard*, October 6, 1964, p. 28.
4. *Ibid.*, November 3, 1964, p. 20.
5. *Faith and Order Trends*, December 1964, Vol. V, No. 1, p. 5.
6. Carol Kleiman, "Resignation and the Rummage Sale," *Renewal*, October 1964, p. 11.
7. Robert St. Clair, *Neurotics in the Church* (Westwood, N.J.: Fleming H. Revell Co., 1963), p. 210.
8. November 17, 1962, p. 37.
9. Roy Kennedy, "Argument," *Macleans*, April 3, 1965, p. 48.
10. "On Being Ordained as a Layman," *Pastoral Psychology*, December 1964, p. 66.
11. New York: Association Press, 1963, p. 16.
12. *Man's Search for Meaning* (New York: Washington Square Press, Inc., 1963), p. 184.
13. *Op. cit.*, p. 52.
14. From Trueblood's introduction to *The Renewal of the Ministry* by Thomas J. Mullen (New York: Abingdon Press, 1963), p. 7.
15. "Letter on the Parish Ministry," *The Christian Century*, April 29, 1964, p. 550.

CHAPTER TWO

1. *The Lutheran Standard*, December 29, 1964, p. 25.
2. Princeton, New Jersey: Princeton University Press, p. 185.
3. "How 'Busyness' Tempts Today's Pastors to Become Frauds," *The National Observer*, January 25, 1965, p. 22.
4. "The Congregation in Mission," *Inner City*, Vol. I, No. 4, p. 1.

CHAPTER THREE

1. Syndicated newspaper column, *Des Moines Register*, December 31, 1964.
2. Arthur Miller, *Death of a Salesman* (New York: Viking Press, 1958).

3. Harry Provence, *Lyndon B. Johnson* (New York: Fleet Publishing Corporation, 1964), p. 31.
4. Richard J. Whalen, "Joseph P. Kennedy. A Profile in Power," *The Saturday Evening Post*, October 10, 1964, p. 32.
5. *Ibid.*, p. 34.
6. September 16, 1962, p. 80.
7. *The Human Problems of the Minister* (New York: Harper & Row, 1960), p. 47.

CHAPTER FOUR

1. *Des Moines Register*, May 17, 1965, p. 2.

CHAPTER FIVE

1. Margaretta K. Bowers, *Conflicts of the Clergy* (New York: Thomas Nelson & Sons, 1964), p. 166.
2. *Des Moines Register*, January 4, 1964.
3. Elton and Pauline Trueblood, *The Recovery of Family Life* (New York: Harper & Row, 1953), p. 79.
4. Betty Friedan, *The Feminine Mystique* (New York: W. W. Norton & Co., 1963).
5. *Des Moines Register*, January 4, 1964.
6. Cf. William Petersen, "The New American Family," *Commentary*, January 1956, pp. 1–6.
7. Marietta B. Hobkirk, "Some Reflections on Bringing Up the Minister's Family," *Pastoral Psychology*, December 1961, p. 30.

CHAPTER SIX

1. Gordon Rupp, *The Righteousness of God* (New York: Philosophical Library, 1953), p. 112.
2. Harold H. Martin, "The American Minister: A National Report on the New Protestant Clergyman—His Troubles, His Triumphs," *The Saturday Evening Post*, April 24, 1965, p. 21.
3. *How To Become a Bishop Without Being Religious* (Garden City, N.Y.: Doubleday & Company, Inc., 1965), p. 2.

CHAPTER SEVEN

1. Walter Wagoner, *Bachelor of Divinity: Uncertain Servants in Seminary and Ministry* (New York: Association Press, 1963), p. 46.

2. As described, for example, in *Spiritual Renewal Through Small Groups,* ed. by John Casteel (New York: Association Press, 1957).

CHAPTER EIGHT

1. Walter Wagoner, *Bachelor of Divinity,* p. 95.
2. *For Self-Examination* (Minneapolis: Augsburg Publishing House, 1940), p. 37.
3. Wagoner, *op. cit.,* p. 96.

CHAPTER NINE

1. "Intelligence Report," *Parade,* February 14, 1965.
2. A. A. Milne, "Binker," *Now We Are Six* (New York: E. P. Dutton & Co., Inc., 1927), p. 18.
3. Wayne E. Oates, "The Mental Health of Ministers," *Pastoral Psychology,* May 1958, p. 7.

CHAPTER TEN

1. Robert Clyde Johnson, ed., *The Church and Its Changing Ministry* (Philadelphia: The United Presbyterian Church, 1961), p. 74.
2. *Ibid.,* p. 81.
3. Viktor Frankl, *Man's Search for Meaning* (New York: Washington Square Press, Inc., 1963), p. 121.
4. *The Philosophy of Nietzsche* (New York: The Modern Library, 1954), p. 709.
5. Edmund Steimle, *God's Incredible Optimism* (published sermon of The Protestant Hour, February 21, 1965).